AGREED!

AGREED!

How to Make Your Management Communication Persuasive

PATRICK FORSYTH

**KOGAN
PAGE**

First published in 1992 by Singapore Institute of Management
and Heinemann Asia
This edition published by Kogan Page in 1993

Kogan Page Limited
120 Pentonville Road
London N1 9JN

© Patrick Forsyth, 1992, 1993

British Library Cataloguing in Publication Data

A CIP record for this book is available from the British Library.

ISBN 0 7494 1050 7

Typeset by DP Photosetting, Aylesbury, Bucks
Printed and bound in Great Britain by Biddles Ltd, Guildford and Kings Lynn

◀ CONTENTS ▶

The Author

Patrick Forsyth is a Partner of Touchstone Training & Consultancy in London. His firm specialises in consultancy and training and the origination of training materials. A consultant for twenty years, he began his career with a major publishing company, has done various sales and marketing jobs and also worked for a professional management institute and an export advisory service.

He is the author of a number of successful management books, including *Marketing Professional Services*, published by Pitmans/ Financial Times, *The Selling Edge*, published by Piatkus Publishing and a humorous guide to demystifying marketing for the layman, titled *Everything You Need to Know about Marketing*, published by Kogan Page. He has also written numerous articles for a variety of management journals.

In addition to his work for individual client companies, he lectures for a number of professional bodies, for the City University Business School in London, and is currently training advisor to a professional body in the travel and leisure business.

◀ PREFACE ▶

This book is about persuasive communication. Now, you almost certainly feel you do not need a book on communication. As a busy manager you communicate all the time – verbally, in writing, with a variety of people – and do so perfectly well most of the time. Occasionally, however, you will find someone asking, 'What do you mean?' in response to something which you have said. Sometimes you initiate the correction – 'But I meant . . .' and sometimes people will say to you 'You want me to do *what*?' As you can see, communication is not always as easy as it seems.

Communication can suffer from being unclear – '. . . you fit the thing onto that sprocket thing and . . .' (just try it). Or imprecise – '. . . then it's about a mile' (three miles later . . .). It can be so full of jargon that we find ourselves referring to a manual excavation device, instead of calling a spade a spade. Or it can be 'gobbledegook'. 'Considerable difficulty has been encountered in the selection of optimum materials and experimental methods but this problem is being attacked vigorously and we expect the development phase will proceed at a satisfactory rate.' (We are looking at the handbook and trying to decide what to do.) So much so that the sense is diluted. There are innumerable barriers to communication, not least the assumptions, prejudices and inattention of those on the receiving end.

All this may simply cause a bit of confusion, and take a moment to sort out or it can cause major problems either immediately or later. Never is there more likely to be problems than when there is an intention to get someone to *do* something. Not only has the message got to be particularly clear but, because the days of saying 'do this' to anyone in most organisations have long since gone, communication needs to be *persuasive*.

Some managers, those in sales or marketing for instance, have to tackle the issue of persuasiveness on a regular basis. But many others do not have this as their 'stock in trade' at all. They are, at base, technical, financial, computer, or administrative people – and may well be very competent in their area of expertise. All have one thing in common – a need to be persuasive. They may not see it in quite those terms, but they need to obtain agreement to get their ideas accepted. This may apply to major factors, like putting a plan of action to the Board of Directors; or to small matters, such as suggesting that a colleague organises things differently to produce, say, more office space for your section. All are important. All demand not just communication, but *persuasive* communication.

Advantages to you. This book is about persuasive communication. You may still feel you do not need a book about communication, persuasive or otherwise. Perhaps not, but how about a book that will help you get your own way more certainly and more often? A book that will reduce the friction of communication breakdowns at work. Something that will help you be seen as a clear, authoritative communicator and, as a result, make those with whom you interact follow your lead. Something that will . . . but, we are jumping ahead. If you are now prepared to reconsider the question of whether you need such a book, please do so now; and, having considered, buy it.

If I have persuaded you to do that, there is a good chance that the book will help improve *your* persuasiveness. Think how useful even a small increase in persuasiveness might be to you, in making things go well in your job.

Getting what you want. The book is in two parts. Part One looks at what makes communication persuasive. This can be difficult enough to achieve, and achieving it can be vitally important to the results you wish to achieve as a manager. But communication can involve greater complexities. The second part examines a main complexity linked to persuasive communication.

Making the best deal. Part Two reviews the techniques of negotiation – bargaining – which is also a communications skill. It overlaps and continues from persuasive communication. Negotiation is concerned with the relationship between two parties where the needs of both are largely in balance. For instance, in the classic case of, say, wage bargaining, the employer wants to reach an agreement (to secure his workforce and keep his business running); and the employees want an agreement (so that the process of negotiation is over, and they can get on with earning at the new rate). This principle of balance of need effectively defines the process. You want a new car. You visit a car showroom. To begin with, you are undecided in your own mind about which model of car to buy. The salesman is therefore, at this stage, selling to you – a process of persuasive communication. (They do not all do so of course, many a car salesman seems not to know his own elbow from his car's exhaust, much less be able to tell you about it persuasively. For a moment, however, keep the ideal situation in mind.) Once you have made up your mind – though you may not tell the salesman this – you are concerned to arrange the best 'deal', the finance, extras, discounts and so on; and the process of bargaining begins.

Simply, persuasive communication is about getting what you want; negotiation about making the best possible deal; getting what you want in the best possible way. So, it is a technique which can help you make better deals. You have no doubt noticed that how people go about the process affects the outcome. The expression which describes a particular manager 'running rings around another' is descriptive of the process. Some always seem to do so, others do not, or do so less effectively. This is because, like so many other things, negotiation is a skill. It can be learnt, to the extent that, with practice, you can be the one running the rings round others. It is a skill which can smooth relations; save you time, money, aggravation and face; one that is eminently worthwhile in many situations throughout business and social life.

Sounds worthwhile? Maybe; but, there is a catch, though not a prohibitive one. It is simply that to be an effective negotiator you need to learn something about the process and the skills it involves, and then practise them. One of this book's objectives is to help you make a start. You need to read it, you need to think about it and practise utilising the principles it sets out. That will take a while, though not too long, but can begin to put you in a position to do better in a number of bargaining situations.

Of course, I want you to buy this book. You want to be more **Is it a deal?** persuasive and an effective negotiator. The book will help you become just that. Buy it and we both get what we want. Is it a deal?

Note It is said that there are two kinds of people in the world, those who worry that the word 'he' only means men, and those who assume it means men and women where appropriate.

I am among the latter, but mean no offence to those in the first category whose fears will not be finally removed until the English Language comes up with a new word with the unequivocal meaning he or she. Alas, there is no such word at the time of writing, so this explanation is offered instead.

◀ ACKNOWLEDGEMENTS ▶

My first job was in publishing, which I joined as what was euphemistically called a 'management trainee'. On a good day, this meant I was a glorified office boy. However, in due course one of the more interesting things I found myself doing was selling books. Now books are a nice enough product to sell, but there are tens of thousands of new ones published each year, so it is not, in fact, necessarily the easiest product to sell; particularly in the days when formal training in the ways of doing so effectively was unusual to say the least.

Only later, having found my way into marketing, marketing consultancy and training, did I begin to understand the psychology of making a message persuasive. In the meantime, I also noticed how many situations in business demand a degree of persuasiveness. It is certainly not only customers who need to be persuaded. The need occurs throughout any organisation. Plans, ideas and proposals all need selling. Just telling people what a good idea you have is unlikely to be sufficient. They need to be convinced.

In writing about this, I am conscious that the process is not something any of us will ever understand completely. Indeed because the techniques involved must be deployed creatively, flexibly, meeting by meeting, person by person; and because the responses from those with whom we communicate will vary and will always be, to a degree, unpredictable, what there is to understand about it changes as we watch.

I am only able to attempt to set out some of the principles which can help guide us because of many past experiences upon which I can now draw. Thanks are due to many colleagues with whom I have worked during my years in consultancy, and from whom I have learnt – and continue to learn – so much. Also to those in the many organisations for whom I have worked on consultancy and training assignments, and those who have been delegates to the courses which I have conducted in the past, from whose shared experiences I have learnt many valuable lessons.

I would also like to thank Joanna Moriarty, of publishers Sheldon Press, for permission to include here certain material adapted from two books of mine which she published, *You Want Me to do What?* and *How to Negotiate Successfully*. Thanks also to my contacts at the Singapore Institute of Management with whom I worked to produce a first version of this book then published as an Asian edition. Though I work regularly in South East Asia it was an interesting experience to be published 'long distance'. And to those at Kogan Page with whom I worked on this book, and whose striking 'Business Action Guide' format I cannot claim to have originated but was pleased to be able to follow.

Patrick Forsyth
Touchstone Training & Consultancy
17 Clocktower Mews
London N1 7BB

Spring 1993

◀ THE PROBLEMS FACED ▶

As a manager you probably spend a major part of your time communicating with staff, with colleagues, with your boss and with others you are meeting or talking to for the first time. Such communication will take various forms from ritual pleasantries – 'Good morning' – 'Have a nice day' – to deep philosophical discussions. On many occasions, perhaps a surprising number of occasions, there is a persuasive intention in the communication.

If things go well, of course, if you have the desired effect, you hardly think about it. And most of the time, it does go well, either because you have a certain inherent ability to persuade or because little persuasion is necessary. When things go wrong, however, perhaps because communication does not occur as you wish, is misunderstood or results either in argument, refusal or inaction – you notice.

Consider the kind of thing that happens. The three case examples that follow, based on real incidents, are typical. They will be referred to again later in the text.

Example 1:

Mr A is the 'number two' in the department. He is having the weekly review meeting with his boss, and is keen to get his boss to agree a change to procedure on a job recently delegated to him. Having carried out the task once or twice, he is convinced he can improve on the way it is done. He expects no problem getting agreement – after all the task has been delegated to him.

Towards the end of the meeting, he asks if he can change the way the job is done. 'But, that's worked well for some years,' says the boss, 'I would need some good reasons – can you tell me in the next sixty seconds why we should change it?' Unprepared for this he mumbles something about perhaps needing to think about it some more, and the meeting is finished.

- Mr A sees a battle looming, has no stomach for it, or is simply unprepared and unsure how to go about it in a way that stands a chance of success, and opts to let things lie. A small incident, but one where the outcome may be simply minor delay, or one where it is now going to be more difficult to raise it in future.

Example 2:

Mr B runs the sales office for a medium-sized company. His team take customer enquiries, offer technical advice, handle queries of all kinds and take orders. Recent reorganisation has resulted in the merging of two departments. His people now occupy a large office together with the order processing staff, who see to the invoicing and documentation. For the most part, all is going smoothly. However, the routing of telephone calls has become chaotic. The switchboard, despite having a note explaining who handles customers in which area of the country, is putting two out of three calls through to the wrong person, and the resulting confusion is upsetting staff and customers alike as calls have to be transferred.

Mr B carefully drafts and sends a memo to the Personnel Manager, to whom the switchboard operators report, complaining that the inefficiency of their service is upsetting customers and putting the company at risk of losing orders. He is surprised to find that far from the situation improving, all he gets is a defensive reply listing the total volume of calls with which the hard-pressed switchboard has to cope, quoting other issues as of far more importance at present to the Personnel department and suggesting he takes steps to ensure customers ask for the right person.

- Mr B intended to take prompt action that would improve

customer service, he felt he had stated his case clearly and logically, yet all he succeeded in doing was rubbing a colleague up the wrong way. The problem remained.

Example 3:

Mr C sits on a management committee. This meets regularly to review opportunities for improvements to quality across inter-departmental boundaries. One of his colleagues is planning to rearrange the office space around the reception area. Whilst making room for an additional person, the change makes the space used for conversations with visitors cramped and possibly noisy. At the next meeting, once 'Any Other Business' is reached on the agenda, he voices his fears and asks the committee to agree to veto the change. There is discussion, argument and conflicting views. After all the pressure on space affects numbers of those present and any change may, ultimately, help pressures in any department. With time pressing, the Chairman suggests they all think about it and the matter is considered at the next meeting.

Three days later the change is made, with a partition removed and a new work station in place.

- Although he had the best interests of the whole company at heart, Mr C has not achieved his aim. What is more, he recognises that it is going to be doubly difficult to make progress at the next meeting now that physical changes have been made.

In each of the preceding examples, basic rules of persuasive communication were broken. In Example 1, Mr A only had a moment to make his point and get agreement. He was not prepared to make his point (perhaps also he did not know how to do so) and the moment passed. Mr B, in Example 2, did think about his communication. He had the customers' best interests at heart, but his note was seen as a personal criticism and he did not get the action he wanted. In Example 3, again the intended end result was not achieved, not least because the problem was not perceived clearly by those at the meeting.

You may like to take a moment, at this point, to consider what else might have been done in each case.

The next section of this book reviews some of the basics of communication, the structure involved which keeps it organised and makes sure it relates to the listener, how to plan and conduct it effectively, and some of the specifics of face-to-face or written communication and the circumstances in which they are used. Then we will return in Chapter 6 to the examples just reviewed.

Overall the intention is to help you structure, simplify and strengthen what you do, so that it is more effective – whilst remaining acceptable to the other person, or people, involved, whose willing agreement you must secure.

With that in mind, we now review the basic principles of communication. As you go through the next section you will find a scrap of paper and a pencil useful as there are some brief exercises to do. It is suggested that you either resist looking ahead to the answers or, having done so, try the questions out on a friend or colleague.

You may like to note any current problem within your own organisation to review as you go through the book:

_____

_____

_____

_____

_____

_____

_____

◀ PART 1 ▶

PERSUASIVE COMMUNICATION

'I am not arguing with you –
I am telling you'

James Whistler

'The ability to express an idea is almost
as important as the idea itself'

Bernard Buruch

◀ CHAPTER 1 ▶

COMMUNICATION – THE ESSENTIALS

Communication – The Basic Objectives

Overall your objectives are simple. Perhaps deceptively simple would be a better way of putting it.

To achieve your purpose, you must concentrate on five communication objectives:

1. to get your listeners to **HEAR** what you tell them (or to **SEE** what you show them);
2. to get your listeners to **UNDERSTAND** what they have heard or seen;
3. to get your listeners to **AGREE** with what they have heard (or to disagree while understanding clearly what you have said or shown them);
4. to get your listeners to **TAKE ACTION** which accords exactly with your overall objective, and which they find acceptable;
5. to receive **FEEDBACK** from your listeners.

Only then will you know if you have succeeded.

Feedback is essential if you are to learn:

- whether they have heard correctly what you have said;
- how much of it they have understood or misunderstood;
- to what extent they agree or disagree with you; and
- whether they intend to take the required action, take some other action or do nothing.

Five Key Objectives.

19

Some feedback is, of course, instantaneously noticeable like 'No' or the dead silence that follows a joke that falls flat. Some may be barely perceptible – a raised eyebrow, which could mean 'I don't understand', '*what?*' or 'No way'.

All this may sound easy enough but in fact, can present a variety of difficulties like transferring an identical message from the mind of one person to the mind of another. The following test is to assess how well you:

1. hear correctly what you are about to hear;
2. understand correctly what you have heard;
3. agree or disagree with what you have heard;
4. act or react to what you have heard.

Four questions for you.

Consider the following four questions yourself, or perhaps try them on a colleague.

Question 1:

Read once and consider very carefully what follows. Then, without lengthy consideration, note down the answer to the question that follows below.

Imagine that you are the captain of a ship which is sailing due north in mid-Atlantic at a speed of 12 knots. After steaming at this speed and in this direction for 30 minutes, the captain gives the order to the engine room to alter course through 180° and then maintain the same speed on the new course for one hour. After another hour, the captain orders the engine room to change course through 180° back on to the ship's original course of due north, 'to avoid a storm'.

Now write the answer to the question, 'What's the age of the ship's captain?'

Is your answer 'I don't know'?

Answer

Most people will read this and write down 'I don't know'. More so if you read it out to them. The reason is that we seem to grow up with the habit of paying least attention to what comes first. We do not, by and large, tend to start concentrating until we are into reading a passage. We tend not to listen to the beginnings of sentences; the beginning of a speech and, most irritatingly, we very frequently do not listen to and get right the name of a stranger to whom we have just been introduced for the first time. Now this is what probably happened to you if, in answer to the question 'What is the age of the ship's captain?' you wrote down 'I don't know'.

Otherwise you would have spotted that '. . . you are the captain of a ship . . .' means **You** who are reading and so the answer is obvious – your own age.

This illustrates quite dramatically that people do not hear correctly what they have just been told. They often do not even listen at all to the first words you say to them.

Question 2:

Follow the instructions below:

Draw, on a scrap of paper, a two-inch horizontal line. Next write the first and last letters of your first name at each end of the line.

Answer

In answer to the above, most people will put the first letter of their name at one end of the line, the last letter at the other, so that Patrick would be represented as P_____K. However what the instruction *actually* said, if accurately followed, would, for the name 'Patrick' look thus: PK_____PK.

Why do we fail to get this right? It is really quite simple. But the question, as posed, did not sound logical, so your mind translated what you actually read into what made more sense, and you put down the result, rejecting what you were actually asked to do.

The communication lesson here is an important one. People will *understand* you correctly if you convey to them your ideas in a way that makes sense to them. It is logical for the first letter of your name to come at the beginning and the last letter to come at the end, isn't it?

Most of the misunderstandings that occur in human communications are due to our failure as communicators to put ourselves in the position of the listener and imagine whether he, she or they will understand what we are about to say.

Question 3:

What is the answer to the question:

$$1 + 1 = ?$$

Answer

Most people, recognising this as a straightforward arithmetical problem, write down $1 + 1 = 2$. Is that what you did? I expect so, like the majority of people. Yet there is at least one alternative answer and there maybe a number of others too. A designer or artist may see it as an artform so, without any hesitation, they will write down $1 + 1 =$ six straight lines.

This reply may be surprising to you, yet is, in a way, as correct as $1 + 1 = 2$. What is the lesson to be learned here? Simply this. Before communicating, we should never assume what people should think, or that a statement is so obvious that everyone will agree with it. It is much better to put ourselves in the position of our listeners and ask: 'How will he receive and perceive what I am about to say or show?'

Question 4:

Write down the first word or phrase (2 or 3 words) which comes into your mind when you hear the phrase 'Paris in the Spring'.

Answer

What did you write down in response to the phrase: 'Paris in the spring'? This evocative phrase has produced thousands of different replies in all parts of the world ranging from the predictable, 'flowers', 'music', 'The Seine', 'love', to others with less obvious associations. There is, of course, no correct answer.

> This highlights another communication lesson. We should always weigh our words and phrases carefully in case they evoke quite different reactions from the one we intend them to produce.

These four communication exercises illustrate that none of the four objectives you aim to achieve are completely straightforward. Let us find out a little more about what causes these communication barriers, and what we can do about them.

You wanted to get people to:

- HEAR what you say (or to see what you show them);
- UNDERSTAND what you mean;
- AGREE with what they have heard;
- TAKE ACTION in accordance with your overall objectives.

Communication – The Main Problems

The first problem is to recognise that, despite what many people believe, communicating successfully is not easy.

Communication can be inherently difficult.

The second problem is to accept that the onus is on the communicator to achieve successful communication, and not on the receiver. In other words, if you initiate a communication which breaks down or is misunderstood, it is, in all likelihood, your fault.

A number of specific difficulties arise that may hinder or prevent the achievement of each objective:

Objectives	Difficulties
● HEAR (or see)	- People cannot concentrate for long periods on the spoken or written word. - People pay less attention to what appears to them as unimportant.
● UNDERSTAND	- People make assumptions based upon their past experience. - Often people do not understand the speaker's jargon. - People misunderstand more easily when they hear but do not see. - People often draw conclusions before we have finished talking.

23

- **AGREE**   – People are often suspicious of others who are persuading them.
  - People do not like being proven wrong.

- **ACT**   – People do not easily change their habits.
  - People fear the results of taking a wrong action.
  - Many people dislike making decisions.

- **FEEDBACK**   – Some people deliberately hide their reactions and what they really think.
  - Appearances can be deceptive – a nod may not always indicate agreement and understanding. It can mask ignorance or indecision.

These difficulties are common to both the communicator and the listener.

If we examine the human communications process, we can better understand how it works, how failures in communication arise and what we can do to be more effective and successful as communicators.

The way we communicate is illustrated in Figure 1:

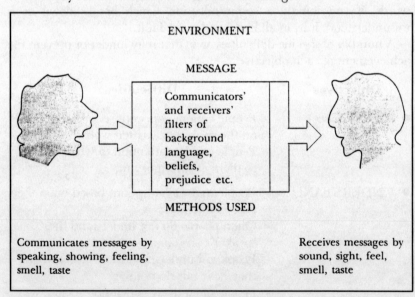

Figure 1   How the human communication system works

Messages are received through our five senses: sound, sight, feel, smell and taste. We then form impressions and assimilate or associate them with other information and ideas stored in the brain. Before we respond to what has been communicated, the brain reacts in a specific sequence to this new information.

It scans existing memories of past experiences and finds the frame of reference or memory which relates most closely to the new information received. The new information is sent to join the existing memory bank or frame of reference chosen.

If it is associated with what that memory perceived, the new information is analysed and subsequently fitted into the existing memory pattern. As a result of this filing system of the brain, the existing memory may:

- remain the same but stronger;
- change for the better;
- change for the worse.

There are constant examples of this memory bank at work. For instance, we may call it up in a listener intentionally by saying 'Remember when . . .'. We know the picture it will paint; or we paint a picture which we hope to conjure up in the listener.

Apart from reinforcing what we believe, other factors influence the quality of our communications. There are five main elements which, as we have seen from Figure 1 can lead to failures in communication: **Five potential dangers.**

- the value standards of the communicator and listener;
- the message being transmitted;
- the filters through which the message passes;
- the methods of communication used; and
- the environment in which communication takes place.

● **The value standards of the communicator and listener**
Our backgrounds, education, beliefs, ethical standards and prejudices all affect the way we communicate with one another. Thus two people looking at the same object or picture or listening to the same story may perceive and react differently. It is thus vital to try to perceive the things you want to say or show through the eyes and minds of the people to whom you speak.

25

● The message being transmitted

The same words may mean different things to different people at different times. Years ago, the word 'gay' meant cheerful, full of mirth, exuberantly merry. Today, it is rarely used in that context but rather as a label for homosexuals. There are distinct differences in the meanings given to English words by the Americans and others. For example, to the Americans there is no such word as *fortnight*; they say two *weeks*; some speak about holidays, Americans talk about a vacation.

Add to these complexities the jargon that frequently creeps into the language of business and special areas of interest, and the result is confusion. As a general rule, avoid – or at least consider carefully – the use of specialised words or jargon. There is a high probability that they will be misunderstood by your listeners.

● The filters through which the message passes

Each person tends to think more about himself than about the people he communicates with, and their words, how they express them and the meaning imparted to them reflect this. Yet their own words, prejudices, beliefs and jargon can set up filters which confuse the message received. Even everyday words can confuse or imply different things to different people. What does it mean to talk about 'older people' – over 60, over 80 or over 20! It depends on your perspective.

● The methods of communication

No two individuals hear, see and feel with equal efficiency. You can tell some people something and they understand immediately. Others have to be told, shown and then asked to play back the understanding of what they have heard and seen before a message gets through.

For this reason when communicating ideas, you should always involve at least two of the senses through which listeners receive a message. You can not only express ideas verbally, but some, including those crucial to your argument, can become more firmly established in your listeners' mind if given visual representation too (like slides at a lecture). Showing something, pointing or referring to something that can be seen or, failing that, conjuring up a good visual image helps.

● The environment in which communication takes place

Any external factor that affects what goes on as you communicate can also influence the outcome. For example, the circumstances of the conversation are also important. If your boss is talking to you in the presence of another senior manager, you will not only be taking in the message but wondering how the other person is taking it in too. Similarly if a father is talking to a child and the mother is there too.

Communication – Making It More Effective

Persuasive communication has something in common with teaching. Teaching (or training) is helping people to learn. Similarly communication is helping people to understand, and persuasive communication is helping people to understand and agree.

Utilising the principles of communication to get your way.

Getting the message over is helped by using the classic rules of learning: effect, forward association, belonging and repetition. Consider these in turn:

- **Effect.** A listener will go along with you more willingly and readily if your message shows how they can satisfy some need they already have in mind. Thus the clever politician does not say 'I am standing on a programme of this, that and the other . . .'; he relates to the basic needs of his audience 'You want jobs to provide money and self-respect, you want . . .' and people are quickly nodding with him.
- **Forward association.** People tend to remember things in the order in which they first learned or heard them, especially if the sequence is logical or if constant reference is made to it. See how much less easily your telephone or car registration number trips off the tongue if you recite it backwards.

This is what the politician is doing when he starts with 'your needs', moves on to what they mean to you and only then discusses how his ideas relate. It is what the salesman does when he identifies that you are interested in low cost motoring, that you want to achieve a high mpg (miles per gallon) and only then tells you about 'the model with the 5 speed gearbox' which has this effect.

- **Belonging.** People understand more speedily and easily what relates (belongs) to their own experiences, e.g. 'an air-conditioner is like a refrigerator element with a fan to circulate the cooled air', or 'the plans I am about to describe are like those you make for your annual holidays'.
- **Repetition.** Contrary to what is often thought, constant repetition

of a fact, a statement or a warning does result in people learning, as pronouncements about dangerous driving, excessive drinking of alcohol, smoking etc. testify. Repetition is only useful as a means of getting people to learn if used in conjunction with one or more of the three rules. A speaker using repetition plus another rule might summarise, by saying 'Let me repeat what I said at the beginning . . .' and restating the same point in different words.

Or to put that in another way, if you repeat key things you want to say, perhaps rephrased, perhaps verbatim, people are more likely to get the message. In other words, repetition is a powerful aid to . . . but you get the idea.

Research shows how people forget what they hear (or read):

- 38 per cent in 2 days
- 65 per cent in 8 days
- 75 per cent in 30 days

and some recall disappears very fast. How much of the TV or radio news do you remember 10 or 20 minutes after hearing it?

But people tend to remember things which are important or of special interest to them. You can help them remember more by:

- ensuring that your first and last impressions upon them are both favourable and positive;
- starting a communication, if it links back to another, by summarising what was said at an early stage;
- giving them a general idea of a proposition before moving on to points of detail;
- involving them from the start by:
  - talking about 'your problems' and 'your requirements' rather than 'what I want';
  - obtaining feedback, so that you know how well you are communicating, and thus can judge whether it is necessary to rephrase your remarks or repeat what has been said earlier;
  - using more than one sense (e.g. speech and sight);
  - planning to communicate (of which more later).

Other considerations
When presented with a proposition to consider, the human mind not

only thinks along certain lines, it is also affected by what it sees and hears. To a lesser extent, the sensations of touch, taste and smell have a bearing on the reception, though sight and sound are of most concern to the listener.

● **Sight** is concerned with your visual impact as a communicator. This may involve overall appearance. There are people to whom a trained communicator like a policeman will say, 'Excuse me, sir,' and others to whom the first words are 'Oi! you.' Or it may be concerned with detail. Is your expression aggressive, determined or understanding; are your gestures adding emphasis or implying desperation? (A good reference on body language is *Body Language* by Allan Peace, published by Sheldon Press.)

● **Sound** is also important. Your voice is characterised by the **tone**, which may be blustering, nervous, urgent, desperate or whatever and also by the **pace** at which you speak. Talk too fast and it can sound glib and insincere, at worst like the archetypal used car salesman. Talk too slow and you sound unprepared, unsure, or nervous. In addition the **emphasis** is important. There is a significant difference between 'You want me to do *what*?' and 'You want *me* to do what?' Lastly you must consider **inflection**. The change of note that puts, for example, a question mark at the end of the sentence.

The opposite of this factor, sound, is of course silence. This is without doubt one of the powerful elements of communication; not what you say but the moments when you stay silent. This reason this is not used regularly is that most people find too much of a pause embarrassing. For them, that is; it may be embarrassing for the other party too, but that is not the reason it is not used. This embarrassment is only psychological, and, in any case, the mind exaggerates it. (Try counting ten slowly, or watching the second hand of a clock or watch ticking away. It seems like forever. But it is only 10 seconds.)

The power of silence.

This is important enough to be worth a couple of examples. A simple one first:

Someone approaches a colleague at work. They are busy at their desk. He asks a question, 'Do you have the file on the publishers Kogan Page?' 'Yes, it's in the file under K.' He points to the cabinet in the corner. 'Can you get it for me?'

Silence.

Who gets tired of, or upset by the silence first may influence what happens next. If the person at the desk sees a need for something to happen first, he may either get up and get the file, or say 'Get it

29

yourself', in a way that may prompt irritation or an argument. If he waits longer, his colleague, not wanting either an argument or a long silence may simply go and get the file first.

Of course, other things altogether may happen, but, if it follows this route, the person at the desk may have to remain silent only 3 or 4 seconds longer to avoid interruption.

Second example, a more pointed use.

A company is considering buying a fax machine. They have had several demonstrations, several quotes and have settled on one as the best buy.

The buyer rings the supplier one more time, and explains that the machine meets their needs, is just what they want in fact . . . but it is a bit expensive – 'Is there anything you can do about the price?' An articulate defence of the price follows, followed by a request to proceed with the deal. The buyer says nothing. The supplier expands on the theme of value for money and ends with another question. Again the buyer says nothing. The second silence is longer, and more awkward. Finally the supplier says. 'Would 10% discount get the order?' and, at this stage, having achieved what he wanted without speaking a word, the buyer agrees.

Easy. At least with an inexperienced salesman at the other end, and although it will not always be that easy, it does show the power of silence.

Summary.

Key points to remember

- Unless someone *hears* what you say, there is no communication.
- You do not communicate just words. The whole person that you are comes with them.
- Talk to people in terms of their own experience and they will listen to you.
- When you have difficulties in getting through to people, it is a sign that your own thinking is confused, not theirs.
- When you fail to communicate, it is not your sentences that need straightening out; it is the thoughts behind them.
- Know what your listeners expect to hear and see before you start talking.
- Your communication is always more powerful if it appeals to the *values* and the *aspirations* of listeners.
- If what you say goes against the beliefs, the aspirations, the

motivations of others, it is likely to be resisted or not received at all.
- It is not what is in your mind that matters – it is what percentage comes across, enters the listener's mind and stays there.

Much of what has been said in the last few pages emphasises that what is important is to consider the listener's point of view, rather than simply putting across *your* point of view. In the next chapter we look at this in greater detail.

◀ CHAPTER 2 ▶

COMMUNICATION – THE STRUCTURE

The Listener's Point of View

You communicate with a wide range of people – family, friends, acquaintances, colleagues at work, and others you know less well. All are individuals. All are different. Some will be amenable to you, others antagonistic, some essentially interested, others unconcerned. All however have a common view, which will help you persuade them; *they consider and decide on whether to agree to something or not in a similar way.*

Abraham Lincoln said, 'When I'm getting ready to reason with a man, I spend one-third of my time thinking about myself and what I am going to say; and two-thirds thinking about him and what he is going to say.' If we understand the process of thinking involved, and relate to it in the way we communicate, it will make our task much easier. Whilst we need to state *our* case, we will only get our way if people on the receiving end find it acceptable. If they believe we are trying to do something *to* them, to persuade them against their will, agreement will be difficult. If they feel we have their interests in mind however, it will be easier.

Understand the other parties' thinking.

Start by understanding the thinking process involved when anyone is considering another's request for action. The process moves through seven stages:

- I am important and I want to be respected
- Consider my needs
- How will your ideas help me?

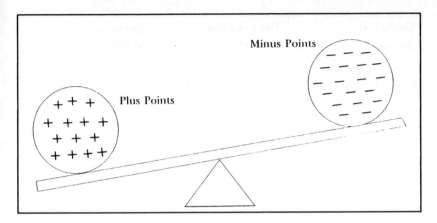

Figure 2   Weighing up the case

- What are the facts?
- What are the snags?
- What shall I do?
- I approve (or not)

This seems like common sense. Indeed if you think about it, you will find it is what you do. A good analogy is that of 'weighing-up' the case or argument, putting all the good points on one side, all the negative parts on the other and assessing the net effect (see Figure 2).

Any attempt that responds unsatisfactorily to any of these stages is unlikely to end in agreement. The mind has to be satisfied on each point before moving on to the next, and to be successful the persuading sequence must match this decision-making sequence, and run parallel to it.

Figure 3 shows the process alongside the persuasive objectives, what you are trying to achieve at each stage, and the technique employed in any communication. The two keys to success are the process of matching the other person's progression and describing, selectively, your case and discussing it in a way that relates to the circumstances of the other person.

When persuasion works, both parties will have gone through this sequence stage by stage. If the attempt to persuade is unsuccessful, it will often be found that:

- the sequence has not taken place at all;

Decision Sequence	Persuasion Objectives	Persuasion Stages
I am important Consider my needs	To create rapport, generate interest or acceptance. To find out about them	1. Opening
What are the facts?	To state a case that will be seen as balanced in favour of action	2. Stating the case
What are the snags?	Preventing or handling negative reactions that may unbalance the argument	3. Handling objections
What shall I do? I approve	Obtaining a commitment to action, or to a step in the right direction	4. Injunction to act

Figure 3   The decision making process

- some stage has been missed out;
- the sequence has been followed too quickly or too slowly, which means the persuader has allowed it to get out of step with the decision process.

As people need to go through other stages, you may not always be able to aim for a commitment to action. You must therefore have some other clear objective on which to get a commitment.

Imagine, for example, that a secretary wants her boss to buy her a new typewriter. The ultimate objective is for him to say 'yes, buy it' about a particular machine. But it may be a step in the right direction to get him to review some brochures, check the quality of what the present machine produces, have a demonstration, get a quote and so on.

Sometimes there are many steps such as this to be gone through before the ultimate objective is achieved.

Consider the objective in your example:

_____

_____

_____

Whatever your objective is, however, it is important to know and be able to recognise the various stages ahead. With any individual contact you can identify:

- What stage has been reached in the decision process
- Whether your sequence matches it
- If not, why not?
- What you need to do if the sequence does not match
- Has a step been missed?
- Are you going too fast?
- Should you go back in the sequence?
- Can your objectives still be achieved, or were they the wrong objectives?
- How can you help the other person through the rest of the process?

Naturally, the whole process is not always covered in only one contact between people. Several meetings or exchanges may be necessary.

If something complicated is involved, it may well be necessary to have numerous contacts to cover just one of the stages before they are satisfied and both can move on to the next stage. Each contact has a sequence of its own in reaching the objectives. Each contact is a part of an overall sequence aimed at reaching overall objectives.

Although you cannot predict exactly how things will go, anticipating the stages as much as possible, having in mind what you want to do, recognising when things are getting off track and working consciously through the whole process is very much part of making persuasive communication work.

This does not mean you must adopt a 'scripted' or parrot-like approach, but that you intend, and plan, to control the direction of, say, the conversation towards a specific objective. It helps to think of this graphically (see Figure 4). Like a captain of a sailing ship, you might take a number of courses, subject to the impact of wind and weather. You have a clear idea of your destination with an imaginary straight line towards it. This allows you to correct and keep on track.

Before moving on to look at how the four main stages can be used to make communication persuasive, there are two other issues which must be touched on. If persuasion is to take place, it is necessary to tackle the communication with a clear eye on the listener and his point of view. In addition, the whole manner of the approach must be such that it comes across as acceptable, and does not – by seeming over assertive or even aggressive – switch the listener off.

The two issues are: **Making the approach acceptable**
Making the approach manageable

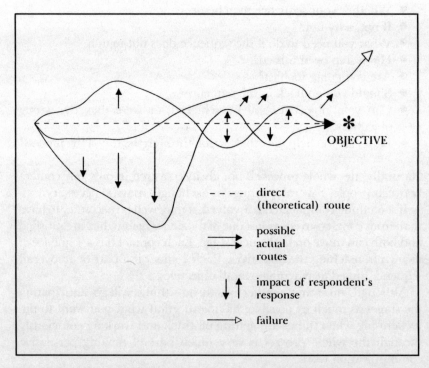

Figure 4   Structuring and directing the communication towards your objective

Making it acceptable

There are two factors that, together, help make your manner accepta-ble. They are an appropriate blend of 'projection' and of 'empathy'. What exactly do these terms mean? 'Projection' refers to the way we come across to others, and particularly the confidence, credibility and 'clout' with which we come over, or at least appear to come over. 'Empathy' is simply the ability to put yourself in the other person's shoes and see things from his point of view. Not only to see them, but to **be seen to do so**.

It is possible to categorise four distinct types of communicator on an axis of high and low projection, and high and low empathy. This is illustrated in Figure 5 below.

Type 1 – the 'high pressure' communicator is over aggressive and insensitive. *They* may feel they win the argument but, in fact, their projection, without empathy becomes self-defeating and switches people off. The archetypal high-pressure person is the popular image of, say, the insurance salesman.

Type 2 – the 'take it or leave it' communicator has little interest in the other person, nor his own ideas. A lack of commitment to the whole process tends to let it run into the sand. The archetypal take it or leave it person is the kind of unhelpful shop assistant with whom most of us are all too familiar.

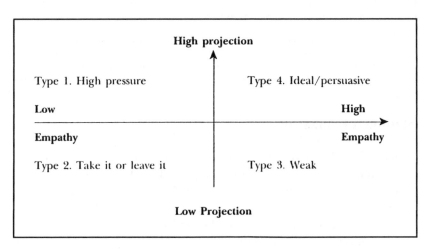

Figure 5   Four approaches to the manner of communication

Type 3 – the 'weak' communicator is one who 'means well'. And so they do. They have good sensitivity to the other person, come across as essentially nice, but take the side of the listener so much that persuasion vanishes and they achieve no commitment.

Type 4 – the 'ideal' communicator is seen as having a creative understanding of the listener, being well-informed and producing both agreement and commitment to the satisfaction of both sides. Being seen to see the other person's point of view is, in itself, crucial.

This is an important balance to achieve. Both elements are important, both can be under or over done. If the combination is right, then it will allow you to do what you want, and the other person will find it reasonable and acceptable. Consciousness of such an approach allows you to fine-tune your approach to produce the right overall effect on the listener.

As we shall see, some of the techniques involved, hinted at already in our examination of the structure are – like the way we ask questions – themselves useful in achieving the right balance.

Consider the potential adverse reactions to the message in your example:
_____
_____
_____

Making it manageable

Effective communication is clear and succinct.

The first element of manageability concerns quantity. Even the best juggler will fail if he tries to keep too many balls in the air at once, and most often, failure means not dropping one ball, but all of them.

The point is well made in a story which, although it concerns a speech rather than one-to-one communication, is entirely relevant to our case.

In his book *The Past Masters*, Sir Harold Macmillan tells of making his maiden speech in the British House of Commons. He spent time carefully preparing it and felt it went well and was received with respect.

Later he was flattered to be approached by a leading politician of the day, Lloyd George, expressing interest in what he had said, but critical of the way he had done it. He persuaded Lloyd George to explain. The explanation ran something like this:

> Never say more than one thing. Yours was an essay, a good essay, but with a large number of separate points. Just say one thing; when you are a Minister two things, and when you are a Prime Minister winding up a debate, perhaps three. Remember your own position. There will be few listeners. What you want is that somebody will go to the Smoking Room and say, 'You know Macmillan made a very good speech.' 'What did he say?' someone will ask. It must be easy to give a ready answer – one point. Of course you wrap it up in different ways. You say it over and over again with different emphasis and different illustrations. You say it forcefully, regretfully, even perhaps threateningly; but it is a single clear point. That begins to make your reputation.

He went on to make other points, but the advice to keep it simple, to boil things back to one, or at best two or three points is excellent advice to any communicator, in whatever circumstances.

It is useful to your thinking to be able to sum up a message in a phrase. Try it with your example:

_____

_____

_____

This brings us to the second element – preparation. The order and clear thinking that achieves three points instead of an essay, that avoids us finding ourselves going through a catalogue which moves from one to another, does not just happen. **Preparation may only mean a few minutes or a few seconds thought, but it must *always* happen.** What needs to be thought through, of course, is the detail of the stages that communication goes through, how it will be done, what may happen along the way and so on.

Communication needs preparation if it is to be effective.

With this in mind we will review the stages – picking up and expanding on numbers of points now made – and then set out a more detailed approach to the process of preparation that will allow you to go through them effectively.

◀ CHAPTER 3 ▶

COMMUNICATION – THE STAGES

Steady as She Goes

Anything we do, certainly if it requires any degree of skill and particularly if we have to fine-tune what we are doing as we go along, benefits from structure. If we are clear in what we are trying to do first, second and next; how each stage relates to the next, then this element of structure becomes, at least in part, reflex and allows us to concentrate on the detail. We have already identified four main stages of the process of persuasive communication (see Figure 3); these are now reviewed in more detail.

Stage one: starting as you mean to go on

Your listeners' attitudes will vary when communication starts, from being welcoming to being downright hostile. Bearing in mind the sequence of decision-making referred to earlier, there are two important objectives:

The importance of first impressions.

- to make the other person feel important, and create the right rapport
- to find out (if it is not clear) what their needs may be.

If you think of other social situations, you will realise that there are many ways in which you can make people feel important and become well-disposed towards you, such as arriving on time, being properly dressed for the occasion, complimenting your host, bringing a small gift with you, and so on. All these social conventions are intended to oil the wheels of personal relationships, and whilst everyone recognises them as such, it does not make them any less useful.

In persuasive situations, similar social conventions apply. The main difference is that they have to be much more carefully used because both parties may recognise them as a means to an end rather than an end in themselves. As a result, the clumsy use of a social convention may be seen as an attempt at manipulation and evoke an adverse reaction. Consequently you have to choose and use these conventions with care. Like other tools they are neutral; it is their use which produces positive or negative effects.

Techniques you can use include:

1. Your general manner

This means your appearance and behaviour. Appearance includes dress and all aspects of your physical appearance from facial expression to finger nails. Make sure your physical appearance and the appearance of anything that will be used is appropriate – a draft letter to be discussed with your boss for instance, will be judged differently if it looks really smart, from one criss-crossed with alterations.

Behaviour includes the usual courtesies like in an office context, waiting to be asked to sit down and using the floor for your briefcase rather than the desk, but it also includes such things as being positive rather than hesitant, enthusiastic rather than diffident.

It is unlikely that you will have problems in this area, but remember that your appearance should create a favourable first impression. First impressions last.

2. Questions and observation

Just as the other person will get an impression of you early in any meeting, so you will want to get an idea of his emotional state. Is he emotionally positive or negative?

One simple way of finding out is to use the normal greeting of 'How are you?', and then really listen to the answer. Is he in a relaxed mood? Has he got enough time to hear your proposals? Is there something else on his mind? Does he want to get down to business straight away or does he want to unwind for a few minutes?

Do not assume that he always wants to indulge in social chit-chat or talk business and nothing else. Circumstances will change and you will need to respond accordingly.

3. Common interests

In persuasive situations, common interests of either a business or a social nature can be used to build rapport with the other person, depending on who they are.

The best ones to choose are those which are topical, relevant to both parties, and germane to the topic of discussion. Focus on the other person rather than you:

> 'What do you think about . . . ?'
> 'How is . . . going?'

In a business context, beware of raising social interests simply for something to say. For example, whilst it is true that many a business deal has been concluded on the golf course, not everyone plays golf, and not all golfers regard a comprehensive replay of a match as a priority during a business discussion.

4. Compliments

Most human beings want recognition and association with success and therefore you can pay the occasional compliment provided that it is *genuine*, not mere flattery, and that it is *specific*, and preferably linked to your relationship with the other person. For example, in an office:

> 'The atmosphere in the typing pool is so much better since we had that word about scheduling the work flow.'

5. Good turns

Starting proceedings with a good turn may cost little in time or money but sets the scene nicely. The loan of a book, a lift to the station, even the offer of a cup of coffee may establish the right rapport before moving on to the real topic of discussion.

6. Reputation

If you are dealing with someone who does not know you, you may need to establish your credentials in terms of experience ('I have been here for more than 10 years'), achievement ('I organised last year's successful meeting'), your understanding of their area of interest or expertise ('I know something of this, because . . .').

There is a danger of getting overly psychological about all this, but used sparingly, such techniques can get things off to a good start.

How the other person's needs can help you communicate better.

The second element of stage one is concerned with relating to the other person's needs. Whilst we may know clearly what they are – although there is always a danger in making too many assumptions – sometimes they need to be unearthed. Indeed whether you discover them accurately and easily can make the difference between an ultimately successful communication and failure.

Making a decision to do something is an action and people act to relieve a felt need. Needs are objectives, goals, ambitions, desires, end results. They are desired effects, not the things that produce them. For example, an engineer wants perfect holes, not precision drills; a householder's objective is to be comfortable, not necessarily to have a particular kind of air-conditioning system.

Thus, people will only act if they have a need, feel it strongly enough to do something asbout it, and believe that the suggested method of satisfying it is worth adopting.

They will not act if they:

- do not have a need;
- have a need but do not feel it;
- have a need, recognise it, but do not feel it strongly; or
- have a need, feel it strongly, but are unwilling to act on it.

Different people will take the same action, but for different reasons, e.g. holidays overseas. Conversely, different people will take different actions, but for the same reasons, e.g. to impress the neighbours.

All decision-making conforms to these basic principles. Sometimes the need is very simple. Sometimes it is intangible, like impressing the neighbours. Always it is an important element in the communication process.

What this means to you is that, from your listener's point of view, he is interested in satisfying his needs, not adopting your ideas. He only becomes interested in your ideas when he sees how they help him achieve his objectives. Then needs and ideas become mutually compatible.

You can only know how to make your ideas attractive to him when you have identified what his objectives are. When he sees that you are interested in identifying his needs, he becomes much more attracted both to you and to your ideas.

So you need to find out.

By getting the listener to tell you his needs and priorities you protect yourself, interest him much more, and obtain a greater success rate in terms of persuasion. It is essential to distinguish between assumed and stated needs. As you listen to another person's statements you must ask, 'Has he stated a desired effect which he wishes to achieve?' Often the unwary will hear a statement and simply assume the need. Until the desired effect has been stated, you have less chance of success.

There are four ways of finding out what is important to the listener:

Finding out what is important to the other person.

1. Think, listen, watch and draw conclusions
The point has already been made about not assuming too much, but with care, the needs may be clearly perceived.

2. Ask questions
This needs to be done carefully, first, in terms of how it is phrased. Ask people 'Are you in favour of smoking whilst praying?' and most people will say 'No'. Ask 'Are you in favour of praying whilst smoking?' and most people will say 'Yes'. Yet the question is actually describing the same thing – the two activities being undertaken simultaneously. So phrase what you ask with real precision.

Secondly, the kind of question itself has a bearing.

There are two ways of asking questions. One is to ask what are called open-ended questions, those which do not permit a 'yes' or 'no' answer, e.g. 'What will the Reception look like when it is reorganised?'

The other more dangerous method is to ask a closed or 'yes'/'no' question, e.g. 'Do you want the Reception reorganised?' Dangerous because they obtain less information, and thus risk your proceeding with a less clear basis of knowledge.

Open-ended questions are preferable for two reasons. First, they allow the other person to develop his own answer rather than putting words into his mouth which he may reject. Second, they encourage him to talk, which at the beginning of a conversation is important. You want a dialogue, not a monologue.

A further technique of questioning must also be borne in mind, particularly in more complex situations. Sometimes questions must probe. You need a sequence of questions to dig for real need-orientated information, thus:

- **Background questions** give you basic information from which you can begin to draw conclusions.

- **Problem questions** begin focus on their situation.
- **Effect questions** help focus on what is happening as a result of the prevailing situation.
- **Need questions** get the person to state needs in their terms.

The sequence that follows, whilst not exactly representing real life, makes the sequence clear:

Where are you?	Up to my neck in the river
Does this pose any problem?	Yes, I can't swim
So what will happen if you stay there?	I shall probably drown
Do you want me to pull you out?	Yes, please

The first answer poses as many questions as it answers, maybe it is a nice day and he is swimming. The last is entirely specific, and puts the rope salesman on the bank in a powerfully persuasive position!

Without this approach you can be perceived rather as the doctor who takes one look at the patient and immediately prescribes a course of treatment. Most of us *prefer* to be asked a few questions in such a circumstance.

3. Statement techniques

When you know the person, or the situation well, perhaps from previous contacts, or if you are just checking interpretation, any statement can have a corresponding question that can lead straight to the moment. As with:

'What will the Reception look like when it is reorganised?' 'Reorganising the Reception will decrease the space for visitors.'

4. Combined questions and statements

This can avoid a string of questions seeming like the Spanish inquisition. A statement of fact and a question about conclusions:

'A reorganised Reception will certainly look different. Do you think it will be a problem?' seem to work best.

The techniques discussed will go a long way to producing stated needs. Sometimes it is still difficult to prompt change, the status quo has a powerful effect. Challenging their previous decisions can make people defensive.

A way round this is by reference to outside factors, things that are not his fault. These may link to other people's actions, materials, or external forces and are, in effect, saying what was the case was fine in the past, but now some external factor calls for a change.

In example two for instance, the fact of the reorganisation may be outside the control of both parties and may prove a useful lever to change 'Because of the reorganisation we must now . . .'.

The last factor to consider, still in what is developing into a complex first stage, is priorities. People may have a need. When they have needs, they will have an order of priorities for them. If we know what those priorities are, we can refer to them in the way we present our case:

'There are many reasons for reconsidering this . . .'
What do you think is most important?

Stage one makes the other person feel important and helps you to find out information that will make the rest of the process easier to achieve. The other person is now at the stage of asking 'How will your ideas help me?' and 'Where are the facts?'

Stage two: Setting out your ideas persuasively

Your task now is to satisfy him on three points, which means that he must find your ideas *attractive*, *convincing* and *understandable*. In addition, you want to be sure that he does find your ideas attractive, convincing and understandable which means you need feedback from him to show this is so. We will now review the techniques for doing just that. As achieving understanding can be regarded as the foundation of the process – it will, after all, be very difficult to persuade someone to a course of action they do not even understand – we will review that first.

People must find what you say attractive, convincing and understandable.

1. Making ideas understandable

To ensure that your ideas have the best possible chance of being enthusiastically received, you need to bear in mind a number of techniques which can improve understanding. These may appear simple, but can, nevertheless, have a disproportionate effect, for example:

Making the méssage clear.

47

- **sequence and structure** – these go together, a logical order, a number of points both linked to the way the other person will see the matter and preferably flagged in advance. As in: 'Let's look at the thing in terms of methods, costs and timing. Shall we start with methods?'

This helps the listener position in his mind what is coming and is appreciated when it relates to his priorities.

- **visual aids** – these are not always appropriate, but are sometimes essential. Consider how you would *tell* someone how to tie a necktie. You can show someone, but try telling them; it is difficult if not impossible. So describe, show and illustrate where appropriate.

- **language** – this must be used so that the other person understands. Avoid words or phrases that may be misunderstood, for example:

'This solution is cheap'
- cheaper than what?
- cheap and, therefore, nasty?

'We offer a 24-hour service'
- available day and night?
- available within 24 hours?
- it takes 24 hours to start and finish?

'I will see to that quickly'
- within the hour, the day, the week, the month?

Many words have both literal meanings and other connotations. Make sure the other person interprets your words in the same way that you do.

Consider what will make the message in your chosen example understandable:
_____
_____
_____
_____
_____

2. Making ideas attractive

You will remember that in Chapter 2, we identified a simple fact of human behaviour, namely that people act to relieve a felt need. The stronger the need, the greater the impact of the solution, favourably or unfavourably. Now, by a combination of questions, statements, and careful listening you have either brought the other person to state his needs or feel you have a clear, factual impression of what they are. At first glance your position and his may seem far apart. Consider an everyday sales example: consider a householder who wants to keep his central heating and water heating costs to a minimum faced with a man selling a maintenance contract which is the most expensive one on the market. The householder cannot see how his costs can be kept down if he buys the most expensive contract. There is apparently no logical connection between his needs and the salesman's proposal, and he would be a fool to accept it. Or would he?

Supposing the salesman could show that the services and checks carried out under the contract are more comprehensive than other contracts and that over the year, the household will spend less on fuel and will not have to pay for any parts that need replacing. The householder may come to the conclusion that this is the best way of keeping his costs to a minimum. In other words, he can now see how the salesman's proposals will help him keep his costs down.

What the salesman has done is to describe what the customer will get out of the contract, and what the contract will do for him. Put simply, the customer can see the desirable results from his point of view of having the most expensive maintenance contract.

Desirable results from the listener's point of view are called benefits. They are what your ideas *will do for your listeners*, not what your ideas are.

People do not buy goods, services, or accept ideas for what they are. They accept them for what they will do for them. Even works of art and antiques are not bought for what they are. They are bought for the satisfaction they give their owners, whether it be visual pleasure, the satisfaction of impressing visitors, or the satisfaction of having an asset that appreciates in value faster than other forms of investment.

Benefits provide the logical link between one person's needs and another's proposals. Benefits are what someone gets out of them; not what you put into them.

What is more, a benefit may not apply equally, or at all, to everyone. A teenager trying to persuade his father to buy him a motor-bike may

Making the message interesting.

A decision to agree will be based on how the other person sees things – not simply on what you want.

49

want a particular model in part because of its performance (a benefit to him), but talk to his parents about its safety features (which produce benefits for them). Benefits may interest people for themselves, for *themselves* wearing a particular hat – as the company accountant, as chairman of the committee; or for *others* – their staff, or colleagues.

People need to know enough about your ideas to be persuaded. They do not want, and often simply do not have the time for a complete catalogue of information about every aspect, large and small, significant or otherwise, of what they are considering. So when you think about your proposals, you may well be able to identify many benefits that can be derived from them; but beware of using too many, believing that the more you say, the more attractive your proposals become. The old saying, 'It's too good to be true' applies here. Too many benefits begin to stretch your listener's credulity.

So, if we have to limit ourselves to one key area upon which persuasion depends (not to exclude others) this is it. People are not persuaded by what something is – called a feature – but by the benefits – what it will do for or means to them.

Let us return to our earlier example of the secretary wanting her boss to buy her a new typewriter. Imagine she studies what is available (no mean task these days) and sets out for him everything about one particular model which is her preferred choice. It is electronic. It has a memory. It has well laid out controls. It is guaranteed and has a good back-up service facility. It is made by a reliable manufacturer. It has the same typeface style as her existing machine, but more options of bold, italic and other graphic devices. She puts this impressive list in front of her boss; but he says 'no'. She asks why, and he quotes the price. 'It is a lot of money.'

Why does this happen? Well, everything she has quoted, along with the price is a feature of the machine. With her understanding of typing the list implies more than it says, but superficially it is unimpressive to the boss; no benefits were mentioned.

Imagine again: undeterred she tries again. This time she says it:

- will allow her to get through 30% more work per hour
- will allow her to present work more smartly and impressively for the customers to whom she writes
- will be low-cost to maintain (and will not, like her old one, spend a significant part of its life in bits, being pored over by a puzzled engineer)

- will match existing documents, and avoid retyping
- can repeat standard documents (saving her time – but that has been mentioned) which will mean they can go out without his checking, saving *his* time, on a tedious job.

This time he says 'yes'. This time she is talking in his terms, about things he can understand, identify with and sees as important. All the points made are *benefits*.

The presentation of a case can be made more effective by combining benefits in a logical sequence which strengthens the case in the eyes (ears?) of the listener. This principle can also be used to summarise:

'This typewriter will improve my productivity, improve the look of the work we send out and impress customers.'

Rarely, if ever, are all the possible benefits catalogued. There is insufficient time, some are less important or are not important to the particular listener in question.

Our secretary friend, on her second attempt above, left out any reference to 'well laid out controls'. This may be important to *her* but not to her boss. All this is not quite as easy to do in practice as it sounds. It is not always as easy as you think to talk benefits, or rather it is easy to lead with features, perhaps because you can easily infer the benefit they produce, and thus think they speak for themselves.

Let us now link the two elements, benefits and features, closer together, then we will consider the precise use of them again.

First, consider what benefits must be in your chosen message:

ACTION

_____

_____

_____

_____

_____

3. Making ideas convincing

Remember the listener is weighing your ideas. He will not just take your word that something is a good idea, in many instances he sees you as having an axe to grind, and may even be suspicious. He wants *proof* that what you say is right. He wants to know *why* that is the case, *how* the effect will be achieved. Of course there are exceptions to this. If your doctor says, 'This treatment will clear the infection in seven days' you will probably not want to know why or how, because you do not need proof. You implicitly accept what he says. Some people build a similar level of confidence with others and can make claims for their recommendations which are never questioned.

Adding proof to your case.

However, you cannot assume that you can state benefits without ever having to substantiate them. Many to whom you speak will view you as having an axe to grind. Therefore, you need to know in what ways your claims can be upheld.

There are three ways of doing this:

- Telling people what they have to do and how they have to do it to obtain the benefits: 'You can increase my productivity and improve the look of the work we send out and impress customers if you buy this typewriter'.
- Mentioning the features involved: 'This machine is much better than the other one *because it is electronic*' (feature).
- Quoting examples of what has gone on elsewhere (third party references): 'You will be able to improve my productivity by 30% (benefit) with the new electronic machine. Mr Bond in Accounts has had one in his department for 6 months (third party), and has saved the cost by reducing his use of temporary staff (benefit).

Features alone are weak. Often you may find this is the bit of an argument that comes to mind most easily, as this is how you see or have learnt about the case. Features used to back up benefits add credibility. Benefits should normally lead, as in point no. 3, but it is possible to state features first using a phrase such as 'which means that . . .' to link the two. There is a danger, however, that in that case an immediate hiatus is introduced, during which the listener is saying to themselves 'So what?', or conjuring up a negative image:

'It is an electronic machine' – 'So what'
– 'Sounds complicated, and
expensive'

So benefits must predominate the argument.

Two refinements to what has been said so far are worth a mention. Benefits can be used as simple statements, and also involved in *comparison statements*:

'This typewriter should improve my productivity by 30%, the next best will achieve only half this.'

Finishing with another benefit produces what is called a *sandwich statement*:

'This typewriter should improve my productivity by 30%, the next best will achieve only half this. In addition, what we send out will be more impressive to customers.'

Finally, in this section, a word about third party references before moving on.

Third party references. These are other people who approve, or have approved, your ideas. They can be powerful persuaders, but you will find them most effective if you follow four simple rules:

Let others help you.

- Use them to support your case, not as arguments in themselves, e.g. 'For example, so-and-so has found . . .', not: 'You ought to do what so-and-so is doing . . .'.
- When mentioning names, make sure they are people or organisations that your listener respects, e.g.
  Supervisor: 'Mr Bond, the accountant thinks it's a good idea.'
  Manager: 'In that case, I'll support it.'
- Choose third parties whose circumstances are similar to those facing your listener, e.g. 'XYZ company in Stirling, which is about your size and similarly organised . . .'
- Do not simply mention the third party. Tell your listener the benefits that the third party obtained, e.g. '. . . Mr Bond in Accounts has had one in his department for 6 months, and has saved the cost by reducing his use of temporary staff.'

Note that throughout stage two (indeed, to an extent throughout the whole process) there is a need to **obtain feedback**.

Persuasive communication is a two-way process. At this stage, you

What do they think?

53

will need feedback from the other person showing that he finds your ideas:

- understandable
- attractive
- convincing

or not.

During the opening of the conversation you will have obtained extremely valuable feedback on needs. Now you need feedback on how he sees your ideas meeting his needs, but your enthusiasm to proceed with your case may prevent you from asking for it or recognising it if offered.

By obtaining and using feedback, you can modify the content, method, and pace of your input. The two methods for obtaining feedback are simple and effective:

Methods of obtaining feedback.

- **Observation**

    Use your eyes and ears to determine his reaction to your proposals. Is he using words, expressions, and actions in response which indicate interest and understanding? e.g.

    'That sounds interesting'
    'Really'
    'I see'
    'Let me make a note of that'

    Is he watching you or gazing out of the window?
    Are his fingers tapping impatiently on his chair?
    Is he beginning to look through his other papers or glancing at the clock?
    Is he leaning forward, obviously paying attention?

    Watch and listen. If you are not getting a verbal response and any body language is unclear, stop talking and wait for a comment.

- **Asking questions**

    If you get neither verbal nor other forms of feedback, you can use a range of questions to elicit specific responses, e.g.

    - to test understanding: 'Have I made it clear how this will work?'
    - to check his appreciation of benefits: 'Do you see how this will make the procedures a lot simpler to use?'

- to check his reaction to a feature: 'What do you think of this format?'
- to check that you are still discussing his needs: 'Is cost reduction what you're mainly concerned about?'

His response to these questions will tell you where you are in the decision sequence and guide you accordingly. By asking them, you will also keep him involved in the discussion and prevent problems later on.

Let us summarise this important second stage before looking at how to deal with negative reactions.

Presenting your case is simple and effective if you follow the basic rules:

- Structure your presentation around others' needs.
- Take one point at a time.
- Tell them what your ideas will do to meet his needs, i.e. talk benefits.
- Show him.
- Provide proof by means of features, examples, and references to others who approve.
- Check your progress by obtaining constant feedback.

Keyrules.

What points will add credibility to your chosen message?

_____

_____

_____

_____

_____

Objections are natural and can in fact help you communicate better.

Stage three: Handling objections

However well you have put your case, it would be naive to assume that agreement will now fall onto your lap, because the other person will, as part of the buying sequence, automatically consider possible disadvantages in your proposal. It is an instinctive response to any situation requiring action, i.e. 'What are the snags?'

If all has gone well, he may not think of any snags, or objections, and move on to the next stage: 'What shall I do?'

If he does think of possible snags, you must be able to answer them to his satisfaction.

Next, we examine objection-handling in some detail. First, you will see why objections arise. Secondly, you will learn how to keep control when this happens. Thirdly, you will learn the particular techniques for handling different types of objection.

Why objections arise

As we have already discovered, people will not normally act without considering the consequences. They may have conflicting needs, such as guests at a dinner party who do not want to offend their host, and therefore keep their jackets on, even if they are feeling very hot and uncomfortable.

But there are other more down-to-earth reasons within your control why objections arise:

- you may not have identified the real needs
- you may have offered your ideas too soon
- you may have talked features instead of benefits
- your benefits may have been too general or too numerous
- you may have failed to obtain or recognise feedback

Thus, many objections are not inherent in people; they are caused by the way a case is put to them. You will reduce the frequency and intensity of objections by communicating well.

How to keep control

The first thing to recognise is that most objections have both an *emotional* and *rational* content. Emotionally, people may become defensive or aggressive! Rationally, they require a logical answer to the particular objection that they have raised. To handle them successfully you will need to tackle the emotional and rational aspects separately and sequentially.

We now investigate how to handle the emotional aspect and keep things under control. The importance of keeping control can be illustrated by the frequency with which current affairs programmes on radio and TV degenerate into slanging matches. If you watch them closely, you will see that the trouble starts when one participant says something with which another disagrees. Instead of controlling their emotions and dealing with the point clearly and logically, they criticise each other. The rest you know only too well.

Keeping emotion under control.

Keeping control is easy if you put yourself in the other person's position when he finds disadvantages in a proposition. If you were him, you would want him to listen to your point of view, to consider it, and to acknowledge that your point was reasonable – even before he answered.

You can do the same with objections raised, keep control, and as a result allow him to consider your answer calmly and rationally.

In conversation it goes something like this:

The other person identifies a 'snag' and voices his objections:

'I think the electronic machine will be too complicated for our needs and, therefore, it is not money well spent.'

You listen; pause; and acknowledge:

'It is a little complicated, of course, compared with what we have at the moment. We have to be sure its better performance makes up for this.'

You will notice that you have not yet answered the objection. All you have done is show understanding of the other's point of view and met the first point in the decision sequence: 'I am important and want to be respected'.

Diagrammatically the situation looks like this:

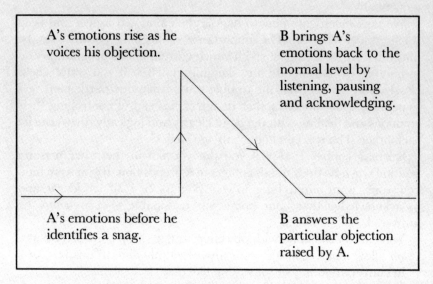

A's emotions rise as he voices his objection.

B brings A's emotions back to the normal level by listening, pausing and acknowledging.

A's emotions before he identifies a snag.

B answers the particular objection raised by A.

So often, rational answers to objections are less than successful because the other person is emotionally unable to evaluate them fairly. By listening, pausing and acknowledging, you keep other people's emotions under control and give your answers the best chance of being accepted.

Whatever the objection there are only three things you can do about it (bearing the weighing up analogy in mind):

- **explain** they are mistaken or incorrect and **remove the snag** from the minus side of the balance
- **explain** they are overrating the effect of it and **reduce the weight** of the snag on the minus side
- **agree.** It is no good trying to persuade them black is white, but **re-balance by stressing benefits**:

  'Yes, the electronic machine *is* more expensive, but it is this kind of machine that allows the productivity improvement I told you about.'

On the other hand objections come in many forms and each may need different tactics.

First, make sure you know what it is you are trying to answer. There is no rule of conversation that says you cannot answer a question with a question; indeed your seeking clarification may well be seen as helpful. A bald question like, 'Isn't it very expensive?' may mean anything from 'No' to 'it is beyond our budget', from 'may be' to '*I* can't decide that'. So check before jumping in.

On other occasions you can use a 'suppose test'.

'Isn't it very expensive?'

'If I can show you how the cost can be recouped through additional productivity, would you be interested?'

If the objection was genuine, the answer may be 'yes'. If it was a false objection, he will have to think of another reason for not agreeing and may say, 'Ah, well, there are other things that I'm not happy about', in which case you can ask what these 'other things' are and deal with them also.

Now let's consider examples of the types of objection you may expect, and examples of specific approaches to dealing with them:

Types of objection and how to handle them.

● Fear objections

Problem. The other person believes that your ideas have unacceptable disadvantages, e.g. 'I do not think the young copy typist would cope with such a complex machine.'

You have to demonstrate that the fear is understandable, but groundless.

Solution. Emphasise elements that will remove the fear – quote examples of similar situations where similar fears have been experienced but did not materialise in the event.

● Habit objections

Problem. Acting from habit is convenient because it can be done with little or no thought. People will not change their habits unless they can see real value in doing so, e.g. 'We have always had simpler machines, I see no reason to change now.' The objective therefore is to give sound reasons from his point of view for reconsidering the situation.

Solution. Emphasise the benefits from your proposal. In severe cases, create dissatisfaction with his present position using the technique described earlier. Then follow with the benefits of your proposal to show that his needs will be satisfied better.

● Wrong information objections

Problem. The other person has been misinformed (or misunderstood your explanation) about some aspect of the idea. He therefore needs to be corrected without being made to look stupid, e.g. 'It won't be compatible with material we already have on disc.'

Solution. Save face 'I am sorry if I gave that impression.' It costs nothing to adopt this approach. Then as you explain the real situation, they will listen without feeling upset.

● Detail objections

Problem. The other person appears to accept your proposal in principle but sees problems in implementing it, e.g. 'I would like to go ahead but it will mean rearranging things a bit as it is a larger machine.'

Solution. Check that the objection is genuine, e.g. 'So if we can rearrange things quickly and simply you'll be happy?' Show him how he can minimise the problems of implementation. Offer to help remove the obstacles. Give examples of what was done elsewhere to show how the obstacles were easily overcome.

● The 'better idea' objection

Problem. The implication is made that something else, perhaps someone else's idea, would be better, e.g. 'We normally prefer to change all the machines in the office together' i.e. a change at a later date would be better.

Your task is to find out why and deal with the real objection behind the comment. This may be fear, habit or some other reasons.

Solution. Ask 'Why?' Depending on the answer, use the appropriate approach to answer the real point.

● Interested party objection

Problem. This may occur where a number of people are involved, and you are perhaps not talking to the right one, 'I can't give you an answer without consulting the office manager.'

Solution. You have to influence the other person, either directly (ask or volunteer to see them) or indirectly suggesting what is, in fact, said to them, i.e. arguments that would appear to their interest.

• Cost objections

Problem. Here there is no, or insufficient, belief that the proposals are worth the money or effort, e.g. 'It is too expensive.' 'It is not worth it.'

Solution. You must establish what is 'value' in the eyes of the other person, so that you can focus on the real need. For instance:

- list (add up) advantages
- show *total* impact e.g. long term as well as short

If it is costly of time, money or effort, the benefits must outweigh the reservation.

Actual cost can be reduced in terms of how they are perceived by amortisation: 'It is only so much *per month*.' Similarly, in terms of time, 'It will take only a few minutes *per day*.'

• Complaints

Finally, there is a category of objection which is a little different, being a complaint based on the past rather than on the current proposition. *Complaints* need slightly different handling:

Problem. The other person feels he has suffered, is annoyed, wants action, and expects you to do something about it, e.g. 'That last report has been with you for three days, and still isn't ready.'

Solutions. Do not make excuses or blame other people – it only makes them feel worse. Follow this sequence:

1. Apologise

2. Ask questions to establish whether the complaint is:
   (a) justified
   (b) unjustified
   (c) emotional

3. If justified
   - apologise again
   - tell him what you will do about it
   - offer to do more than the minimum
   - thank him for bringing it to your attention

4. If unjustified
   - apologise again
   - save his face (he may be in the wrong)
   - explain what he or both of you can do to prevent a recurrence

5. If emotional
   - apologise
   - save his face
   - wait until he has cooled down

To summarise, 'What are the snags?' is an instinctive part of the decision-making process. By the time someone reaches this stage, he should be sufficiently attracted by your proosal to pass through it without raising objections.

Successful communicators concentrate on objection prevention, not objection cure.

Your knowledge, perhaps from previous meetings with the person, may help, or your research highlights what objections are likely to be raised. As you think about possible objections and how you can either anticipate them or prevent them from arising, the following may help your memory and thus your preparation. Just remind yourself of the four arithmetic signs and how they can prompt a useful line of argument:

+ add up the relevant benefits to minimise the advantages;
- spell out the worries one by one that can be subtracted from the person's mind;
÷ divide any snag by reference to the times they will benefit from your idea;
× multiply the benefits by choosing those that will satisfy the needs completely.

By agreement on stated needs and careful selection and presentation of need-related benefits, you can successfully reduce both the number and strength of objections.

Successful handling of objections depends on:

- **keeping the emotional atmosphere under control;**
- **identifying the real needs behind the objections;**
- **using the appropriate technique.**

Consider what objections your chosen message is likely to prompt and how you can handle them:

_____

_____

_____

_____

_____

Stage four: Injunction to act

Getting agreement.

You are not always after the ultimate agreement, as was mentioned earlier, you are – or should be – always after agreement to a definite step on the way. In effect you are after achieving:

    – your ultimate objective;

or – an interim objective.

In either case, of course, if the other party willingly accepts your suggestions, there is no need to actually ask for agreement to act. They are more likely to do so if you had identified, explored, and agreed on the needs. Then in stating your case you put forward your ideas in an attractive, convincing and understandable way and if objections were raised, you kept control and answered them to the other person's satisfaction.

Attempts to get a commitment without first having created a desire for the proposal will normally be seen as pressure tactics. The bigger the decision, the greater the pressure, and the stronger the resistance. Nobody likes to be pushed to what they see as an inappropriate degree.

Asking for agreement does not *cause* agreement to happen. It merely converts high desire into agreement and low desire into refusal. Even when desire is high, a positive commitment may not be volunteered. Similarly, people may want to make a commitment but there are several variations of it, and you want one particular kind.

It is in these situations that your skills have to prompt an injunction to act. In all cases, however, successful communicators recognise that people act to relieve a felt need. They therefore concentrate on the advantages to be gained from a positive decision rather than on the decision itself.

At the stage where the question 'What shall I do?' is being asked, you first need to be able to recognise that this stage has been reached – spotting the signals that make it apparent – and secondly to use different techniques, essentially just different ways of asking the final question, to suit different people and situations appropriately.

Signs of agreements

Reading the signals.

Sooner or later the person to whom you are speaking will reach the stage of asking himself 'What shall I do?' At the worst, he will quickly reject your proposals. If so, you have to identify why and act accordingly. However, he will more often be interested and you will see this interest in his actions or words. Such signals will include:

- tone of voice, posture, hesitation, nodding;
- questions on details showing acceptance in principle;
- comments expressing positive interest, attraction etc.

These can be converted into agreement, e.g.

'What is the delivery time on the electronic machine?'
'Well, if you give the go ahead I can have it in and working for the week after next.'

Often when people commit, they take a risk. They are not absolutely sure that they are doing the right thing. You can increase their confidence at this stage by continuing to stress the advantages. Otherwise you simply have to ask. This is actually a stage you can find yourself avoiding. You say things like 'Is there any more I can tell you about this?' or 'Is that all the information you want at this stage?', when you should be saying, 'Right, are we agreed?' or 'Let's do it.' There can be almost an embarrassment about asking which leads to this avoidance. You very much come to the point where there is no more to be said, where the only thing to do is to ask for agreement. The only remaining decision for you concerns the right way to phrase the question.

The following illustrate a number of different approaches:

• Direct request

Just ask: 'Shall I place an order for this one?' A secretary could use this with a boss who likes to make his own decisions. It does run the risk, of course, that he may say 'no' or 'I'll think about it.' If he does respond in this way, she must ask 'Why?' or 'What do you want to think about?' so that she can deal with it and close again.

Approaches to getting agreement.

• Command

Some people find it difficult to come to a decision or have considerable respect for your judgement and respond better to an instruction than a request. For example, 'Let me put the order in today, and we will quickly have every typed sheet going out of the office looking more impressive.' In this case a command linked to a benefit.

• Immediate gain

There will be occasions when, by acting fast, people can obtain an important benefit, whereas delay may cause them severe problems. When this happens, you can use an 'immediate gain' to encourage them to take an early decision e.g. 'If you do let me order it today, we will have it to type the Forsyth proposal which must be out by the end of the month.'

• Alternatives

Sometimes you will realise that there are a number of options, any of which is acceptable to you. By offering these alternatives, you give the other person the opportunity to choose his preferred option. For example, 'Shall I order the basic machine or the one with the enhanced memory?'

By alternative, we mean a 'yes' or 'yes' question, *not* something which ends '. . . are you going to do this, or not?' and poses a negative alternative.

• Third party reference

During your discussions you may find that the other person is particularly impressed or reassured by the fact that another organisation or individual whom he respects has benefited from your recommendations. If so, you can refer to it as you ask the final question, using any of the other techniques, 'We can duplicate Mr Bond's experience and improve productivity in this department within a week or two. Shall I place a firm order?'

• Summary

If the idea you are putting over is complex; or in comparison with another (or several), is better in some respects, but perhaps not in others; this method is useful. You simply summarise the key issues and link to a question:

> 'This machine will give us the productivity improvement, improve presentation and will be reliable. Shall I confirm the order?'

• Assumption

Sometimes things have gone so well that agreement really can be assumed. In this case you can run the conversation on, *as if yes has been said*:

> 'Fine, once we have dealt with this morning's post, I will get on to the supplier and place an order.'

This leaves the other person able to agree very simply with a nod or a brief 'yes'.

ACTION

How, in your example, will you phrase the final question?

_____

_____

_____

_____

_____

That is all there is to it. Each stage, process and technique is simple by itself. If there is a complexity to it, it is in orchestrating it all together. This is helped by preparation.

◀ CHAPTER 4 ▶

PREPARING TO COMMUNICATE

Be Prepared

A prerequisite for success.

Good ideas, however sound and well argued, however convincing in their own right, must be put across attractively, clearly and persuasively. By now it will doubtless be clear that this does not just happen. The person who you admire as articulate, who you think of as having the 'gift of the gab', is in fact normally the one who has thought about it beforehand. He is the one who makes a habit of so doing, who is *prepared* to communicate. Preparation is only a grand word for a bit of thought. Engage brain before mouth or writing arm. You only need to think back to the last time you said to yourself 'Why did I ever say that?' to verify that a moment's thought is often what makes the difference between success and failure in communications.

No clever techniques are involved, just avoid jumping in with both feet when you should be thinking about it first. Sometimes this is a second or two, as conversation with someone proceeds. A pause is perfectly possible. Just a sentence in response to a question for instance – 'Well, I must think about that', 'That's a good point' – gives you a second or two for thought. You may surprise yourself with just how much thinking can go on in a second or two, if you do it *consciously*.

On other occasions, it needs some real thinking through. Beforehand, a few notes may help. Or a word with a colleague or friend or both. This kind of formality is more natural perhaps with written communication. If you have an awkward letter to write, draft it roughly first. Start with a few words, move to a rough draft, then write the final letter. There is no reason why this cannot, in effect, happen with other kinds of communication too.

A meeting with a colleague is looming, even two or three minutes spent quietly with a scrap of paper will help organise your thoughts. You will make it most effective, and quickest, if you go about it systematically. There are, in fact, four sequential stages:

How to prepare.

(i) Set your objective – decide what you want to achieve. This may seem simple and clear. 'I want the boss to increase my salary.' How you go about achieving it may be more straightforward if the objective itself stands up to some analysis.

The objectives should be SMART meaning specific, measurable, achievable, realistic and timed. Consider how this applies to the objective stated above in one short sentence.

Is it _specific?_ Well, yes as far as it goes. But what do you mean by salary? Would inclusion in the annual bonus scheme, an upgraded company car (or a car if you do not have one), or some other addition be acceptable? You need the full picture in mind.

Is it _measurable?_ More is, perhaps technically, measurable. £1 added to your annual salary is more. An extra day's wages because it is leap year is more. What do you mean? Ten per cent more, £1,000 more? Define it in your mind, not exactly perhaps, but at least in terms of some definite options.

Is it _achievable?_ £10,000 more would be nice, but is it likely, in your wildest dreams, to be agreed? Set your sights – and your specific objective – on something realistic.

Is it _realistic?_ If 'achievable' means 'can I get this?', realistic means 'should I?'. How will asking for an unreasonable amount be seen? Will it make you a laughing stock, or mark you down as a trouble-maker? What you ask for needs to be viewed in this boarder way to make sure it is realistic.

And how about **_timed_**? Do you want the increase this month, next month or at the end of the year? After the results for your section are in, or before? How many meetings, or conversations are you prepared to take, over how long a period to achieve your aim? A memo, a meeting, another memo, another meeting, or more?

This kind of thinking, analysis if you will, can pay dividends. It clarifies in _your_ mind what you are after and will help ensure that everything that follows is best designed to achieve it.

69

(ii) Do background research - like planning, this is a grand description for a straightforward task, though one which, on occasions, will take a few minutes. Ask yourself what you need to know, to check, to look up, before embarking on this communication. Staying with the same example, if you want a raise, do you have the record of when you have had increases, and how much they were? Do you know what the trends are in your kind of business for salary levels? What is the organisation's policy and salary structure? What is happening with inflation and the economy?

In considering these issues, some overkill may be necessary. In part you are saying what you will *definitely* need at your fingertips for this meeting, in part what you *might* need.

(iii) Think through the meeting - particularly the structure. How will you start? How will you state your case? What evidence, examples or illustrations will you use? How will you phrase the final question?

You need to anticipate, but not assume, some of the feelings on the other side. Will your boss be pleased by or hostile to the request? If the latter, what responses will you use and so on.

(iv) Decide what you will need with you - this sounds an obvious statement but it is easy either to leave a note, perhaps of a key figure, behind as you go to the meeting; or be unable to locate it in the bundle of papers you do take. The latter will be read as someone in a muddle, or less sure of his ground. This stage will include consideration of, not just notes, but physical objects, a calculator in our running example for instance.

Make no mistake; all this is vital. Good communicators make it look so easy. Silver-tongued and confident, they apparently have no problem getting across what they want and achieving their objectives. This is deceptive. The so-called 'born' communicator is often simply the person who consciously thinks about what he/she is doing (perhaps, in part, as the result of some study) and, more specifically, who plans what he/she is going to do in advance.

It is a process that not only organises what follows better for the listener, but builds your confidence - and if you are to be persuasive you must have, or appear to have, confidence - because you know it is well organised and can thus work more easily.

Now, you can begin to prepare your example message:

_____

_____

_____

_____

_____

_____

_____

_____

_____

_____

_____

_____

◀ CHAPTER 5 ▶

COMMUNICATIONS METHODS

More Than One Way

So far in the text, there has been an assumption that most communication is verbal and face-to-face. And indeed it probably is. This is not the only way to communicate, however, and whilst it raises issues that may be worthy of more separate study, we will now consider the differences imposed by different methodology, and specifically those of communication by telephone and in writing, both of which are routinely used by most managers. Some of the points made may seem obvious, but the point is rather – do they make a significant difference to how we need to communicate and the chances of success? In some cases the answer is very much in the affirmative, and the differences necessary should not be underestimated or overlooked. In addition, some of the principles set out here apply equally to face-to-face communication.

On the telephone

Any telephone conversation is simply two-way communication, albeit using a particular medium. It is surely not difficult, after all some people will talk on the phone for hours. On the other hand, like any communication, there may be a good deal hanging on it. Any problem will dilute the chances of success. And the problems of 'voice-only' communication are considerable, and in some cases prohibitive. Try describing to someone how to tie a necktie for example – without any gestures or demonstration. It pays therefore to consider all the factors that can make vocal communication successful.

Voice-only communication.

These are perhaps best reviewed in terms of how you use the telephone itself, your voice and manner, obtaining and using feedback, and planning. The telephone electrically distorts the voice, exaggerating the rate of speech and heightening the tone. You must talk into the mouthpiece in a clear normal voice (if you are a woman, it helps to pitch the voice lower). It is surprising how many things can interfere with the simple process of talking directly into the mouthpiece: smoking; eating; trying to write, holding a file or book open at the correct page and holding the phone, sorting through the correct change in a call box; allowing others in the room to interrupt or allowing a bad quality line to disrupt communication (it is better to phone back). All so obvious yet so easy to get a little wrong, thus reducing the effectiveness of communication.

Voice and manner
Remember that on the phone, you have to rely on your voice and manner in making an impression. None of the other factors of personality are perceptible. Here are some suggestions to help you:

- **Speak at a slightly slower rate than usual**
Speaking too rapidly makes it easier to be misunderstood and also mistrusted, although speaking too slowly can make the listener impatient or irritated.

- **Smile. Use a warm tone of voice**
Though a smile cannot be seen, it does change the tone of your voice. Make sure you sound pleasant, efficient and, perhaps most important, interested and enthusiastic about the conversation. Enthusiasm is contagious.

- **Get the emphasis right**
Make sure that you emphasise the parts of the communication that are important to the listener or for clarity. Only your voice can give the emphasis you want.

- **Ensure clarity**
Make sure you are heard, especially with names, numbers etc. It is easy to confuse S's and F's for instance, or find 15 per cent taken to mean 50 per cent.

- **Be positive**

Have the courage of your convictions. Do not say: 'possible', 'maybe', 'I think' or 'that could be'.

- **Be concise**

Ensure a continuous flow of information, but in short sentences, a logical sequence and one thing at a time. Watch out for and avoid the wordiness that creeps in when we need time to think, e.g. 'at this moment in time' (now), 'along the lines of' (like), they can confuse or distract.

- **Avoid jargon**

Use as little jargon as possible. Whether it is company (e.g. abbreviated description of a department name), industry (e.g. technical descriptions of products, processes), or general (e.g. phrases like 'I'll see to that immediately' – in 5 minutes or 5 hours? 'Give me a moment – literally?'). If you have to, at least check that the other person understands. He may not risk losing face by admitting you are being too technical for him, and a puzzled look will not be visible. Jargon can too easily become a prop to self-confidence.

- **Be descriptive**

Anything that conjures up images in the mind of the listener will stimulate additional response from someone restricted to the single stimulus of voice.

- **Use gestures**

Your style will come across differently depending on your position. For example, there may even be certain kinds of call that you can make better standing up rather than sitting down, e.g. debt collecting or laying down the law. (Really. Try it, it works – this alone could cover the cost of this book many times over!)

- **Be natural**

Be yourself. Avoid adopting a separate, contrived, telephone 'persona'.

Your intention is to prompt the other person into action. You should speak naturally in a way that is absolutely clear. The following are some useful rules.

- **Be clear**

Make sure the message is straightforward and uncluttered by 'padding'. Use short words and phrases. Avoid jargon.

- **Be natural**

Do not behave or project yourself differently.

- **Be positive**

Be helpful in tone and emphasis.

- **Be courteous**

Always be courteous.

- **Be efficient**

Project the right image.

- **Be personal**

Use 'I' – say what you will do.

- **Be appreciative**

'Thank you' is a good phrase.

Obtaining and using feedback

- **Talk *with* people, not at them**

As a first step to encourage response, form a picture of your listener (or imagine them if you know them) and use this to remove the feeling of talking to a disembodied voice.

- **Remember to listen**

Do not talk all the time. You cannot talk and listen simultaneously.

- **Clarify as you proceed**

Ask questions, check back as you go along – it may appear impolite to ask later.

- **Take written notes**

Note down anything, everything, that might be useful later in the conversation or at subsequent meetings. Get the whole picture and avoid the later reaction of being told 'but I said that earlier'. Do it as you proceed, not at the end of the call.

● **Maintain a two-way flow**
Do not interrupt, let him finish each point – but make sure, if he is talking at some length, that he knows you are listening. Say 'Yes', 'That's right' to show you are still there.

● **Concentrate**
Shut out distractions, interruptions and 'noises off'. It may be apparent to your listener if you are not concentrating on him – it will appear as lack of interest.

● **Do not overreact**
It is easy to jump to conclusions or make assumptions about a person you cannot see – resist this temptation.

● **'Read between the lines'**
Do not just listen to what is said but what is meant. Make sure you catch any nuance, observe every reaction to what you are saying.

Planning

The importance of 'engaging the brain before the mouth'.

Because we are attempting to gain agreement or commitment, planning the call is important.

This does not mean a lengthy period of preparation, though certain calls may be well worth planning more formally, but it does mean the brain must always start working before the mouth! Making a few notes, a few moments' thought before dialling is usually worthwhile. This kind of planning will help you:

- overcome tension or nervousness
- improve your ability to think fast enough
- prevent side-tracking or being side-tracked
- make sure you talk from the listener's point of view
- assess your own effectiveness

and above all, it will help you:

- to set clear and specific objectives designed to gain agreement and a commitment from the other person.

Planning is necessary even to cope with in-coming calls (at least those that follow a pattern). It is designed to make sure you direct or control the conversation without losing flexibility and react to others accurately, without being led on by them. (Remember the sailing ship in Figure 2, it is the same principle that keeps you on track.)

Finally think about when and where you will make key calls – from a call box or an open plan office? If they are important it is worth organising a timetable of when/where calls can be made. Plan to make difficult calls early and do not put them off – they will not get easier, rather the reverse.

Never think of any call as 'just a phone call'.

How you sound

People considering their effective use of the telephone should know how they sound to a listener at the other end of the line. **Listen to yourself.**

This is not difficult to organise; a standard cassette recorder or dictating machine on which you can record your own voice is all that is necessary. The result will be very similar to what you would hear on the telephone.

Practise simply by talking and playing back. Rehearse on any particular important point for calls which you know you have to make.

Better still, get a friend or colleague to hold a conversation with you so that you hear yourself, on playback, responding to questions and conversation that you are not expecting.

If you have not done this before it is likely that even a few minutes of self-analysis will show you a lot, and allow any specific weaknesses or habits to be improved. The same applies, of course, to members of your staff and such practice makes good sense at departmental meetings.

In writing

Letters last. Unlike telephone calls (which are not often recorded) they stick around to be re-read and reconsidered. They need to look neat, think with what trepidation you start reading something that is illegible or untidy. Some may be worth getting typed to ensure the look that is necessary. **Putting the message down on paper.**

No matter what the subject of the letter is, we want to be sure that our letters will (a) command attention, (b) be understood, and (c) be acted upon (it is this that differentiates persuasive communication from simple factual communication). If they are to do this, we have to take some care

77

in preparing them; in this age of dictating machines and rush and pressure, it is too easy to just 'dash them off'.

The same is true of any written communication, like proposals, reports and so on, so often management is not simply passing on information. There is an objective, something to be achieved and this must be put persuasively. Of all the tasks carried out, writing is the most likely to get 'in a rut', with long established style and form, being reiterated ad infinitum.

If you doubt this effect, look at a number of documents that have gone out of your office recently and read them - objectively - with a fresh eye. How would you see them if you were on the receiving end? Are they clear, straightforward, and above all, are they persuasive where necessary?

We will use letters as an example of the approach to writing, bearing in mind that the same principles form the basis of composing more complex documents.

Preparing persuasive letters

Before you put pen to paper - think!

Before we even draft a letter, we should remember the sequence of persuasion, and in particular remember to see things through the other person's eyes. Then we should ask ourselves five questions:

- For whom is the letter and its message intended? (This is not always only the person it is addressed to.)
- What is/are his/their particular needs?
- How do our ideas or propositions satisfy those needs - what benefits do they give?
- What do we want the reader to do when he receives the letter? We must have a clear objective for every letter.
- How does the reader take this action?

The last two questions are frequently forgotten, but they are very important. It should be perfectly clear in our own minds what we want the recipient to do, and very often this can be put equally clearly to the reader; but having achieved this, we can lose the advantage if lack of information makes it difficult for them to take the action we want.

The most important part of a letter is the first sentence. It will determine whether the rest of the letter is read. People seldom read a letter in the same sequence in which it was written. Their eyes flick from the sender's address to the ending, then to the greeting and the first sentence, skim to the last. If the sender is lucky, the reader returns back to the first sentence for a more careful reading of the whole letter. So the first sentence is about the only chance we have of 'holding' the reader, and it should arouse immediate interest. But gimmicks should be avoided. They invariably give the reader the impression of being talked down to. So how can we achieve the best opening?

Write out the name of the person you are writing to. Seeing it written down will help you visualise his point of view. When possible, always address the letter to a person rather than to 'Dear Sir'. It is much less formal, everyone likes hearing his own name, and unless we write 'personal' on the envelope, there is no fear that the letter will lie unanswered in his absence. Keep references short and subject headings to the point – his point.

Make sure the start of the letter will (a) **command attention** (b) **gain interest**, and (c) **lead easily into the main text**. For example:

What the letter *must* do.

- **a**sk a 'Yes' question.
- **t**ell him why you are writing to him particularly.
- **t**ell him why he should read the letter.
- **f**latter him (carefully).
- **t**ell him what he might lose if he ignores the message.
- **g**ive him some 'mind bending' news (if you have any).

The body of the letter runs straight on from the opening. It must consider the reader's needs or problems from his point of view. It must interest him. It must get the reader nodding in agreement – 'Yes, I wish you could help me on that'.

In drafting, we write down what we intend for him and list the benefits, not just features, and in particular benefits which will help him solve that problem and satisfy that need.

We have to anticipate his possible objections to our proposition in order to select our strongest benefits and most convincing answers. If there is a need to counter objections, then we may need to make our letter longer and give proof, e.g. comment from a third party that our benefits are genuine. However, remember to keep the letter as short as possible.

Our aims are:

- To keep the reader's immediate interest.
- Keep that interest with the best benefit.

- Win him over with a second benefit (or more).
- Obtain action at the end.

In drafting we can make a (short) summary of the benefits of our proposition to him. Having decided on what action we want the reader to take, we must be positive about getting it. It is necessary to nudge the reader into action with a decisive final comment or question, just as was advocated in face-to-face contact.

A word about language
Remember our intention is to prompt the other person to action rather than demonstrate our 'Oxford English', (though it is nice to be grammatically correct – an excellent, readable, and amusing guide is the book *English our English* by Keith Waterhouse, Viking, 1991). We should write much as we speak.

Some basic rules for written communication.

Be clear
Make sure the message is straightforward and uncluttered by 'padding'. Use short words and phrases. Avoid jargon.

Be natural
Do not behave or project yourself differently just because it is in writing.

Be positive
In tone and emphasis (be helpful).

Be courteous
Always.

Be efficient
Project the right image.

Be personal
Use 'I' – say what you will do.

Be appreciative
Thank you is a good phrase.

You may find it will help you examine specific aspects of the language you use in letters (and elsewhere) to review the following list and find alternatives:

Avoid trite openings

We respectfully acknowledge
  receipt of   _____

I have to acknowledge with
  thanks   _____

Yours of even date to hand   _____

We have pleasure in attaching   _____

Referring to your
  communication of   _____

The contents of which are noted   _____

This letter is for the purpose of
  requesting   _____

If we follow the rules for a good opening, we shall also rarely begin with 'Thank you for your letter of'.

Avoid pomposity

We beg to advise   _____

The position with regard to   _____

It will be appreciated that   _____

It is suggested that the reason   _____

The undersigned/writer   _____

May we take this opportunity of   _____

Allow me to say in this instance   _____

Which you claim/state   _____

For your information   _____

Having regard to the fact that   _____

We should point out that   _____

Answering in the affirmative/
  negative   _____

We are giving the matter every
  consideration   _____

We are not in a position to   _____

The opportunity is taken to
  mention   _____

Despatched under separate cover   _____

Avoid coldness and bad psychology

Advise/inform   _____
Desire   _____
Learn/note   _____
Obtain   _____
Regret   _____
Trust   _____
Your complaint/dissatisfaction   _____
Dictated but not read by   _____

Avoid cliché endings

Thanking you in advance   _____
Assuring you of our best
   attention at all times, we
   remain   _____
Regretting our inability to be of
   service in this matter   _____
Trusting we may be favoured
   with   _____
Awaiting a favourable reply   _____
Please do not hesitate to   _____

Keep it simple – use short words to the following long ones

Additional	_____	Duplicate	_____
Alteration	_____	Elucidate	_____
Anticipate	_____	Emphasis	_____
Appreciable	_____	Encounter	_____
Approximately	_____	Endeavour	_____
Assistance	_____	Envisage	_____
Beneficial	_____	Facilitate	_____
Considerable	_____	Finalise	_____
Consequently	_____	Fundamental	_____
Commencement	_____	Generate	_____
Cooperation	_____	However	_____
Deficiencies	_____	Immediately	_____
Despatch	_____	Implementation	_____
Discontinue	_____	Initiate	_____
Discussion	_____	Locality	_____

Manufacture	———————	Optimum	———————
Materialise	———————	Practically	———————
Merchandise	———————	Purchase (verb)	———————
Necessitates	———————	Problematical	———————
Nevertheless	———————	Requirements	———————
Numerous	———————	Sufficient	———————
Objective	———————	Termination	———————
Obtain	———————	Utilise	———————

Use one or two words rather than several

According to our records   ————————————————

A large majority of   ————————————————

A percentage of   ————————————————

Along the lines of   ————————————————

At a later date   ————————————————

At this precise moment in time   ————————————————

Due to the fact that   ————————————————

Facilities are provided for   ————————————————

Generally speaking in this
    connection   ————————————————

I am inclined to the view that   ————————————————

In the event that the foregoing   ————————————————

In the initial stages   ————————————————

In the neighbourhood of   ————————————————

In the not too distant future   ————————————————

It is not possible to effect delivery   ————————————————

On the occasion of   ————————————————

Prior to this, we experienced
    trouble with   ————————————————

There can be no doubt about   ————————————————

The position will soon be
    reached that   ————————————————

Should the situation arise that we
    are unable   ————————————————

We are prepared to admit   ————————————————

We shall not be in a position to   ————————————————

With a view to/in order to   ————————————————

With regard to   ————————————————

With the result that   ————————————————

Finally, on a lighter note, two further examples. First, if you use cables, telex or even fax, and have an eye on the cost, be careful of abbreviating too much. There is a story of a journalist, writing a show business feature, who cabled Hollywood for information. His message read 'HOW OLD CARY GRANT'. In due course the reply came back 'OLD CARY GRANT FINE. HOW YOU?' Secondly, watch for the language of bureaucracy creeping into reports, memos, and longer documents. The much circulated 'Standard Progress Report', found on many a company notice-board, makes the point, taking three impenetrable paragraphs to make a few simple points. (See Figure 6.)

Throughout the whole process, bear in mind exactly who you are going to be communicating with, always have their characteristics very much in mind. Is it someone you know well? – where a good mutual understanding exists and you can get straight to the point without too much preliminary. Is it someone with the same understanding of the topic of discussion as you? – in which case no elaborate explanation is necessary. Is it someone senior, older or more important than you? Someone who will expect, or appreciate, a little respect? Are they going to be difficult? (Do you know this or are you assuming it?) and if so do you need to be that much more careful, polite or circumspect? Will they be (rightly) upset by what you want? If so, do you break the news gently or get straight down to it? There are few rules here, but most problems occur not because you cannot handle the situation, but because you have not taken enough time and trouble to think it through and adapt your approach to the circumstances.

Winning them over. There are however techniques that will get people on your side, listening and more likely to take notice of you. All involve a respect for the other person and their point of view:

Standard Progress Report

For Those with No Progress to Report

During the survey period which ends 14 February, considerable progress has been made in the preliminary work directed towards the establishment of the initial activities. [*We are getting ready to start, but we have not done anything yet.*] The background information has been surveyed and the functional structure of the component parts of the cognizant organisation has been clarified [*We looked at the project and decided that George would lead it.*]

Considerable difficulty has been encountered in the selection of optimum approaches and methods but this problem is being attacked vigorously and we expect the development phase will proceed at a satisfactory rate [*George is looking through the handbook*]. In order to prevent unnecessary duplication of previous efforts in the same field, it was necessary to establish a survey team which has conducted a rather extensive tour through various departments with immediate access to the system [*George and Henry had a nice time visiting everyone*].

The Steering Committee held its regular meeting and considered rather important policy matters pertaining to the overall organisational levels of the line and staff responsibilities that devolve on the personnel associated with the specific assignments resulting from the broad functional specifications [*untranslatable – sorry*]. It is believed that the rate of progress will continue to accelerate as necessary personnel are made available for the necessary discussions [*We will get some work done as soon as we find somebody who knows something*].

Figure 6   Standard Progress Report

1. **Relate to people something important** – take them into your confidence, involve them.
2. **Praise as often as possible** – Let people feel ideas are their own – and that they are important/worth considering.
3. **Give freedom of action** – be open-minded about possible mistakes.
4. **Listen to people with sincerity** – show interest in their interests.
5. **Create involvement in (major) tasks** – include them in team, or group activity.
6. **Ask for advice or opinion** – and show respect for their ideas.
7. **Give credit** – show up the results of their efforts in front of others.
8. **Give them a sense of responsibility** – support them in discussions with others, let them feel.
9. **Delegate tasks – agree main objectives** – let them work out details.
10. **Be courteous to them in all activities** – help in defining problems.

Much of this, of course, comes down to giving some time to work things through, to create a relationship that will be workable, both ways. Because modern life is, for many people, one long rush, communication problems occur simply because insufficient thought went into the process.

◀ CHAPTER 6 ▶

THE CASES REVISITED

A Successful Conclusion

Now, in light of all that has been said, let us return to the cases that
appeared in the Introduction and see how the principles discussed apply
to these situations.

In each instance, the example is restated to avoid referring back and
then a suggestion, in terms of a more persuasive approach, is made. Bear
in mind that there are no 'right' answers, no certainty that a particular
approach will guarantee success. The suggestion sets out an approach
that appears to be well-matched to the circumstances, and therefore
would stand a higher chance of success than the original action taken.
Let us take them in turn.

Example 1:

Mr A is the 'number two' in the department. He is having the weekly
review meeting with his boss, and is keen to get his boss to agree a change
to procedure on a job recently delegated to him. Having carried out the
task once or twice, he is convinced he can improve on the way it is done.
He expects no problem getting agreement – after all the task has been
delegated to him.

Towards the end of the meeting, he asks if he can change the way the
job is done. 'But, that's worked well for some years,' says the boss. 'I
would need some good reasons – can you tell me in the next sixty seconds
why we should change it?' Unprepared for this, he mumbles something

about perhaps needing to think about it some more, and the meeting is finished.

This is a prime case of a battle lost before it began. The answer lies largely in preparation.

Mr A would have known, if he had thought about it first, that

- he wanted to make a change
- it might be difficult to achieve this, or at least need some discussion
- any problems of communication are compounded by lack of time, and in such a meeting by lack of forewarning (an agenda?) and a prepared case.

On the other hand, he has time on his side, he can afford to take a moment to get it right, and think it through before the meeting.

So, what could he have done, having thought about it? His objectives are clear, but he needs the manager on his side and must introduce the question at the right moment and in the right way. What he in fact did, introduced it at the easiest moment for the manager, who unsurprisingly perhaps seemed to rate his life being kept uncomplicated and the status quo being preserved highly, to refuse.

Maybe the conversation should have started more like this:

'I would like to show you how we can improve efficiency in the department, by making a minor procedural change – may we allow time in the meeting for me to run over it with you and see what your view is?'

An opening designed to make it clear that it is a positive area, likely to be useful and worth the time needed to discuss it; and that contains a small element of flattery ('. . . what your view is?')

Once the principle of discussion is agreed a, preconsidered case can be put – and the manager is likely to be in a mood to listen and consider.

Perhaps the case is best preceded by some questions:

'Would it be useful if we could reduce the time this takes?'
or perhaps focusing on the effect of so doing:
'If we could save time on this we would be better placed to get the improvement you want in customer service, wouldn't we?'

This makes clear that one of the manager's objectives may be met as a result of the conversation rather than it being a subordinate 'wanting something', and something that will take up valuable time, the focus is on the manager's needs.

In these circumstances agreement to discuss, and perhaps to agree the matter (the latter will depend, of course, on the case put forward) is much more likely. It illustrates how minor differences, in this case in the way the matter is introduced, can potentially have a major effect on the outcome.

Having got Mr A sorted out, let us turn to Mr B and his problem with the office switchboard.

Example 2:

Mr B runs the sales office for a medium-sized company. His team take customer enquiries, offer technical advice, handle queries of all kinds and take orders. Recent reorganisation has resulted in the merging of two departments. His people now occupy a large office together with the order processing staff, who see to the invoicing and documentation. For the most part all is going smoothly. However, the routing of telephone calls has become chaotic. The switchboard, despite having a note explaining who handles customers in which area of the country, is putting two out of three calls through to the wrong person, and the resulting confusion is upsetting staff and customers alike as calls have to be transferred.

Mr B carefully drafts and sends a memo to the Personnel Manager, to whom the switchboard operators report, complaining that the inefficiency of their service is upsetting customers and putting the company at risk of losing orders. He is surprised to find that far from the situation improving, all he gets is a defensive reply listing the total volume of calls with which the hard-pressed switchboard has to cope, quoting other issues as of far more importance at present to the Personnel department and suggesting he takes steps to ensure customers ask for the right person.

- Mr B intended to prompt action that would improve customer service, he felt he had stated his case clearly and logically, yet all he succeeded in doing was rubbing a colleague up the wrong way. The problem remained.

Here the core of the communication is in writing. The memo Mr B sent, though well-intentioned, had the wrong effect, and would also have made any follow-up conversation (necessary because the problem had still to be resolved) more difficult.

From the way the example is first stated, we can imagine the sort of memo that was sent, probably something along the following lines:

Memorandum

To: Ms X, Personnel Manager   3 March
From: Mr B, Sales Office Manager

Subject: Customer Service

A recent analysis shows that, since the merging of the sales office and order processing departments, two out of three incoming calls are misrouted by the switchboard and have to be transferred.

This wastes time and, more important, is seen by customers as inefficient. As the whole intention of this department is to ensure prompt, efficient service to our customers, this is not only a frustration internally, it risks reducing customers' image of the organisation and, at worst, losing orders.

I would be grateful if you could have a word with the supervisor and operators on the switchboard to ensure that the situation is rectified before serious damage results.

The problem is certainly identified, the implications of it continuing are spelt out, a solution – briefing of the relevant staff by the Personnel Manager – is suggested. The intention, as has been said, is good. However, despite a degree of politeness – 'I would be grateful . . .' – the overall tone of the message is easy to read as a criticism. Further the solution is vague, tell them what exactly? It seems to be leaving a great deal to Personnel. Maybe he felt 'it is not my fault, *they* should sort it out'. To an extent this may be true, but you may find you often have to choose between a line which draws attention to such a fact or which sets out to get something done. They are often two different things.

In this case the key objective is to change the action, and to do so quickly before customer relations are damaged. This is more important than having a dig at Personnel, and worth taking a moment over. It is, whilst a matter of overall company concern, something of more immediate concern to the sales office.

So what should Mr B have done? To ensure attention, collaboration and action, his memo needed to:

- make the problem clear
- avoid undue criticism, or turning the matter into an emotive issue
- spell out a solution
- make that solution easy and acceptable to those in Personnel (including the switchboard operators themselves)

Perhaps with that in mind, his memo should have been more like the following:

Memorandum

To: Ms X, Personnel Manager   3 March
From: Mr B, Sales Office Manager

Subject: Customer Service

The recent merger of the sales office and order processing departments seems to have made some problems for the switchboard.

You will find that I have set out in this note something about what is happening and why, and specific suggestions to put it right. You will see the suggested action is mainly with myself, but I would like to be sure that you approve before proceeding.

Memorandum

The problem
Two out of every three calls coming in are misrouted and have to be transferred. This wastes time both in my department and on the switchboard and is likely to be seen as inefficient by customers. To preserve customer relations, and perhaps ultimately orders, it needs to be sorted out promptly.

The reason
Apart from the sheer volume of calls, always a problem at this time of the year, the problem is one of information. The switchboard operators have insufficient information to help guide them, and what they do has been outdated by the departmental merger. Given clear guidance neither they, nor customers, will have any problems.

Action
What I would suggest, therefore, are the following actions.

i) I have prepared a note (and map) showing which member of staff deals with customers from which geographic area, and would like to make this available for reference on the switchboard.
ii) This might be best introduced at a short briefing and if we could assemble the operators for ten minutes before the board opens one morning, I could do that with them and answer any questions.
iii) Longer term, it would be useful if the operators visited our department and saw something of what goes on, we could arrange a rota and do this over a few lunch hours so that it can be fitted in conveniently.

If this seeks a practical approach do let me know and I will put matters in hand.

Like Example 1, this is not set out as the 'right' or guaranteed approach, but it is certainly better. And it is more likely to work because it follows the rules, right back to the seven steps set out in Chapter 2. Specially:

- it lays no blame
- it recognises that Personnel, and the switchboard are important
- it considers their needs – for clear guidance, being able to handle the volume more easily, someone else taking the action
- it anticipates objections, who will do all this, for instance
- it is specific in terms of action, who will do what.

There seems every chance it will have the desired effect. Many situations exhibit similar characteristics. All it needs is a clear, systematic approach that recognises the other person's point of view.

Now let us review Mr C's situation in a similar way.

Example 3:

Mr C sits on a management committee. This meets regularly and is concerned to review opportunities for improvements to quality across inter-departmental boundaries. One of his colleagues is planning to rearrange the office space around the reception area, in a way which whilst making room for an additional person, makes the space used for conversations with visitors cramped and possibly noisy. At the next meeting, once 'Any Other Business' is reached on the agenda, he voices his fears and asks the committee to agree to veto the change. There is discussion, argument and conflicting views. After all the pressure on space affects numbers of those present and any change may, ultimately, help pressures in any department. With time pressing, the Chairman suggests they all think about it and the matter is considered at the next meeting.

Three days later the change is made, with a partition removed and a new work station in place.

- Although he had the best interests of the whole company at heart, Mr C has not achieved his aim. What is more, now the deed is done, he recognises that it is going to be doubly difficult to make progress at the next meeting now that physical changes have been made.

Like any matter of 'territory' this is certainly a potentially emotive issue. It has to be discussed, amongst a number of people, in a short space of time. One at least of those is potentially likely to see the whole thing as 'anti-me'. So it needs careful handling. Maybe Mr C should speak to one or two other committee members before the meeting to ascertain their views. Maybe he could talk to someone, in a different area, who has faced the same problem; to, say, 'office services' so that they understand the technical possibilities for accommodating the people and equipment involved. All this, and no doubt other things, might help.

What, in any case, are the objectives? To stop any change? (Probably not realistic). To ensure his total requirements are met? (Yes, but can agreement on that be achieved in the time?) To delay any change until there is agreement in principle as to how to proceed? (That may be more achievable). Propose a compromise alternative? (Is something that might be acceptable all round possible?)

Let us imagine he opts for delay. Then his approach might have been as follows.

- some 'homework' as referred to above
- once the item is raised, to make it clear immediately that he wishes to make sure any change is carried out in the best interests of all those affected (including customers)
- to set out something of the problem, enough to get agreement that it is something to take a moment to consider (a pre-briefed allies' agreement will be helpful here)
- a specific suggestion as to action – this much delay, these checks, discussions in the meantime – another meeting (when?) to decide.

Perhaps even the instigator of immediate change would see this as reasonable, and again objectives are achieved.

These three cases are snapshots, typical of so many everyday situations in business, where persuasive communication is necessary. They do not include every factor that can come up, and what is suggested in the way they are reviewed is not set out to provide the basis for any sort of 'script'. When situations are not stock, but always individual, stock responses are not, in any case, the answer.

What is illustrated is the way of approaching similar cases, showing something of the techniques that can be deployed, something of the structure that must be followed and the thought and preparation that is necessary. The latter, in the end, boils down to the simple premise

'Ready, aim fire!', stated in these terms any other order is clearly less likely to be effective.

Make any final notes here about how you will make your example message work:

_____

_____

_____

_____

_____

_____

_____

_____

_____

_____

PART 2

MAKING THE BEST DEAL

'When a man tells me
he is going to put
all his cards on the table,
I always look up his sleeve'

Lord Hore-Belisha

◀ CHAPTER 7 ▶

THE BASICS OF BARGAINING

Foundation Stones for Successful Bargaining

Communication – making something clear – is never easy. Persuasive communication – getting someone to do what we want – can be downright difficult and negotiation – agreeing the 'deal' – is something else. Before we get into the details about negotiation, we must set the scene and recap, briefly, on the basic skills from which it springs because negotiation is an added dimension to communication. The two are at once separate processes, and inextricably linked.

Persuasive communication may demand negotiation.

As we have seen in Part One, communication may *seem* deceptively easy. Whatever form it takes, it may run into problems because it is unclear, or imprecise, or full of jargon. There are dozens of potential hazards ranging from you losing the thread of your argument, to the other person not listening. One more classic example of communication breakdown is, perhaps, worth quoting before we move on. A good one is the story of the journalist cabling Hollywood, as part of the research for a show business feature, with the message 'How old Cary Grant?' The reply comes back 'Old Cary Grant fine. How are you?' You can probably think of many more personal examples of such confusion.

If people do not understand exactly what you mean, you cannot hope to move on to the next stage – of *persuading* them.

*Clear communication is the first foundation, indeed the first stage, of the total process.

If communication is clear, then it is quite possible to make that communication *persuasive*. This, in turn, is dependent on the right approach. And this must be based on the point of view, and thinking, of the *other* person. It is very easy for communication to end up unpersuasive because it is no more than our saying 'do this', with no consideration of the other person or their point of view. Action is what we are after, but action taken ultimately because the other person understands, appreciates and sees the need for it.

This is all especially true for most managers, in most companies, with lack of time being a prime enemy of clear communication. The more you have on your plate, the more important details of communication tend to be skimped, and the greater the chances of confusion. If persuasion or the greater complexities of negotiation are involved, the dangers are increased. The concept of the listener's point of view was reviewed in Part One and is crucial to communication in general, and to negotiation as well.

Thus:

*Persuasive communication, successful persuasive communication, is thus the second foundation for successful negotiation.

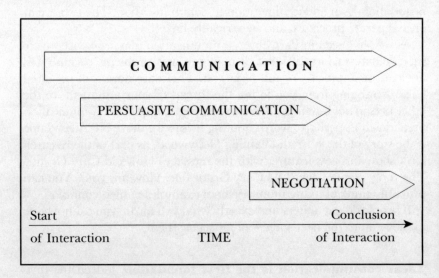

Figure 7   The communication overlap

Only when someone is persuaded towards a particular form of action, at least in principle, will they be interested in moving on to make any sort of deal.

So if you have communicated clearly and achieved understanding, if you have succeeded in being truly persuasive and there is essentially agreement to proceed, then you can move on to the process of negotiation.

In real life the processes overlap. There is no sharp division. Often a complete cycle of interaction takes place as shown in Figure 7, with communication, of course, going on throughout.

Whilst the approach described, operating from the basis of a sound appreciation of the other person's point of view, is the beginning of effectiveness in this area, there is clearly more to it than that. The process of communication needs working at, that of persuasive communication even more so. It must be made manageable. It needs planning, structure and to be deployed with an acute consciousness of what is going on, if only because it must be deployed interaction by interaction as we never know – in dealing with people – how they will react.

To say more here would be to repeat Part One of this book. Though if you are dipping into the book, let me urge you to read Part One first, as negotiation works best when communication is clear and persuasion has been achieved.

So, with this in mind, we will turn now to the more detailed consideration of negotiation as such, and start by looking at some of the basics.

You may like to have a topic you know you will have to negotiate on in future in mind as you read on, if so note details here:

_____

_____

_____

_____

_____

_____

_____

_____

◀ CHAPTER 8 ▶

THE MAJOR ELEMENTS OF NEGOTIATION

Assembling the Techniques

Let us begin with what negotiation is not. It is not just stating a grievance. If you have a complaint – say the toaster has come back from the menders and is still doing a good impression of a crematorium – it is somehow instinctive to complain without proposing a remedy. At best, complaints produce apologies. At worst arguments in which threats produce counter threats, and, too often, an impasse. Too often, much company communication is of this nature. It starts with a complaint – 'Productivity in your department is dropping', 'Sales results are below target' – and deteriorates into argument – 'No, it's not', 'There are good reasons for that'. What we really want in such circumstances is action. We have to put up, or encourage, a proposal which will put things right. Arguments cannot be negotiated, only proposals can. This demands that emotion is kept under control. Negotiation is a delicate process which needs thinking about carefully, both before it occurs and whilst it is taking place.

Often negotiation fails because it does not take place. People may be afraid of the process. We look for an easier way which in fact, tends to become a confrontation and then deteriorates into an argument which leaves no one satisfied.

It is inherent to the process of negotiation that *both* parties end up feeling satisfied that an appropriate deal has been struck. This characterises a description sometimes put on negotiation, that it is a 'win-win' situation. Of course, some negotiators do take a much less

The concept of the 'win-win' deal.

constructive approach and go for what one might well call a 'win-lose' objective, determined to win on every point at all costs. A better outcome is usually likely through the 'win-win' approach.

'Win-Win' means:	
– the emphasis should be on seeking common ground	(rather than fighting for your way on everything)
– relating to the other party and their concerns	(rather than just objecting to them)
– you must be ready to compromise, at least to some degree	(rather than the opposite)
– discussion must accommodate to and fro debate	(rather than insist on a rigid agenda)
– discussion should include questioning (and therefore listening)	(rather than just statements of our case)
– appropriate disclosure of information should take place and openly stated point of view	(rather than secretiveness)
– building relationships between the parties is important	(rather than bad feelings)
– we aim for agreement	(rather than stalemate)

What follows assumes we normally aim for a 'win-win' style negotiation rather than an argument.

The complexities of negotiation demand a careful approach.

Negotiation is a complex process, in that there are a number of different elements that need to be borne in mind if it is to progress satisfactorily. Negotiation is the process of identifying, arranging and agreeing the 'terms and conditions' of a deal. Persuasive communication starts the process during which one party puts across his case and the other begins, in his own mind, to accept it. As agreement in principle begins to be accepted, the question switches from '. . . will this person agree?', to 'on what basis will he agree?', and both parties are concerned that the deal agreed on each and every detail will suit them as much as possible. It may be impossible for both to be satisfied 100% on every factor but the balance must be right.

The different factors, or 'variables' as the jargon of negotiation has it, may be many and various, and this contributes to the complexity of the process. Consider an everyday example which makes this point.

Imagine you are going out to make some major household purchase – a refrigerator perhaps. Which model you buy, and from where, is dependent on a number of factors; perhaps a surprising amount. There is price, of course. But there are also a number of factors about the fridge itself; the star rating of its freezer unit, the size, number of shelves, bottle holding capacity, the colour, which way the door opens, and so on. There may be other, less visibly obvious factors; how much does it cost to run, will they deliver (and in how long, and with what certainty), what payment terms are available, what guarantee and service arrangements apply – you can no doubt think of more.

Now this kind of a purchase may simply involve checking, and considering such factors and then making a decision. That may be complicated enough. But the factors may not be fixed, that is the shop either offers them or not, but some have to be suggested and negotiated. You only get certain things included in the deal when they have been raised, discussed and agreed. And, what is more, balanced. This means both parties may need to give as well as take. You agree to delay delivery by two weeks, they will then deliver free of charge – when they have a van coming your way. They agree to knock 10% off the price, if you agree to pay cash. And so on.

The variables are the raw materials of negotiation. Each has a scale of possible decisions on which we must settle and agree. Discount – none or 50%. Delivery – this afternoon, this week, next week, sometime . . . More of this later. For the moment we note that there are often many of them, and that we have to have a clear idea of what part of the scale is likely to be acceptable to us, and of their respective importance.

It is the number of these factors often inherent in a negotiation situation, coupled with the variety of human interactions involved that make it complicated.

If we are not careful, we may look back and find we lost out. If we do not even recognise what is to be done at negotiation, then we handle it inadequately and end up feeling we have got a raw deal. For example, the administration manager telephones to complain about an incorrectly completed service on a company car. A complaint may prompt an apology. But no more. If he wants something done about it, he must negotiate a remedy. From a practical point of view, there is a considerable difference in approach, and in the likelihood of getting suitable redress. If we see something as negotiation but go at it like a 'bull in a china shop', or focus exclusively on one element, or allow the transaction to develop into an argument, then we are unlikely to do as well as we could.

The fundamentals of success.

There are three, inter-related, **fundamentals** upon which success in negotiating rest. **The first is *what* you do** – the techniques and processes involved. **The second is *how* you go about it** – the manner employed and the effect this has on those with whom you negotiate. **And the third**, on which the first two are inevitably dependent, **is *preparation*.** Consider the last first. To prepare for negotiation seems logical and common sense. Yet more negotiators fail to make a good arrangement than they might, for want of adequate preparation than perhaps for any other reason.

This raises two important points. First, success in negotiation, like so much in life, *does not just happen*. Of course, people who have some skill in this area tend to make it look simple. This again is true of many skills, an accomplished public speaker or a good cook both make what they do look easy; but this does not mean that a good deal of preparation has not been necessary before that impression can be given. So, accepting that preparation is necessary is the first step to making what you intend to do successful.

Secondly – and perhaps this compensates in some measure for what you may see as a chore – sound preparation can give you your first 'edge' in negotiation, and certainly can, regardless of other effects, give you a head-start in comparison with another who has skimped in this area.

Make no mistake, such an 'edge' may be very necessary. In many kinds of negotiation no quarter is given, a great deal may be hanging on the outcome and the negotiator needs to have every 'trick of the trade' on his side to give him an edge. The following story (reproduced from my earlier book *Everything You Need to Know about Marketing*, Kogan Page, 1990) perhaps illustrates the point:

'It is any buyer's job to get the best possible deal for his company.

That is what they are paid for, they are not actually on the salesman's side, and will attempt to get the better of them in every way, especially on discounts.

This is well illustrated by the apocryphal story of the fairground strongman. During his act, he took an orange, put it in the crook of his arm and bending his arm squeezed the juice out. He then challenged the audience offering £10 to anyone able to squeeze out another drop.

After many had tried unsuccessfully, one apparently unlikely candidate came forward, he squeezed and squeezed and finally out came a couple more drops. The strongman was amazed, and, seeking to explain how this was possible, asked as he paid out the £10 what the man did for a living. "I am a buyer with Ford Motor Company," he replied.

Buyers are not really like this; they are worse.'

It is not just buyers, of course. So too may be whoever it is you are negotiating with, they will be intent on fighting their corner, meeting their objectives and will do their best for them; not you.

So it makes sense to review what preparation for negotiation entails and how you go about it.

Preparation

If, for the moment, you consider yourself inexperienced at, and perhaps even afraid of the thought of negotiating, remember this is, in part, only because you are ill-prepared for it. Being well-prepared breeds confidence. Confidence allows the process to be managed better than an ad hoc approach. Appearing confident is read by the other party as competence (and the way we appear is very important as we will explore later).

As with all communication, preparation is key.

So, we must prepare. What does that imply? Preparation may be just a few moments' thought prior to the start of a conversation; it may be a few minutes or an hour or two of homework; or it may, in an industrial or business context for instance, be days of discussion and rehearsal. Whichever it is – it must *always* take place.

There are several headings under which preparation can be considered.

How to prepare.

The people involved

First, we should consider the person, or people, with whom we must negotiate and, if appropriate, the organisation they represent. Negotiations take place with all sorts of people, customers, suppliers, business colleagues – the boss, subordinates, and so on.

The first step is to ask ourselves some questions about them. What role or intentions do they have? What needs (subjective or objective) might they have? What problems will they raise? What objections? Are they in a position to make a decision or must they consult someone else?

Each different situation will raise different issues, but the principle of thinking through how people may handle something is similar in each case.

Suppose you are making the arrangements with the Banquet Manager at an hotel for an important occasion like the annual company meeting. You want it to go well. You want it to be appropriate. You want it to be memorable. He wants it to go well too, of course; but he also wants it to fit in with other functions, to be easy to staff and to be profitable. The different perspective means you must be sure the Banquet Manager is in sufficient authority to make the arrangements you want, that he is professional and knowledgeable about the things that need to be done and that what he says will be possible, will actually be there on the day. Suppose he suggests a combination of rooms A and B. You feel B and C would suit better. Is his suggestion based on how your party will be best accommodated or to allow him to fit the local Football Club in room C? And do you want them next door in any case? As each element such as cost, catering etc. is discussed and various options reviewed, what you know of the Banquet Manager and his intentions will allow you to negotiate better with him. You may never have met him before, but some consideration of his point of view will always help; as it will with whoever you have to deal with.

The other party involved is, of course, you. How he sees you is important too. He will respect you more if he feels you are professional (expert, if circumstances make this appropriate), if you clearly have the authority to negotiate, if you appear prepared, confident and in-charge. You will never actually be as close to the ideal in these respects as you would like but very often the other person has no way of knowing this and appearance is, in a sense, the right word. Some people have the confidence to tell you black is white and make you believe it. The exception to this is appearing prepared. You must, as has been said, actually be prepared (though it does no harm to let people think you are even better prepared than you are). This also means thinking about other matters in advance.

> **What must you bear in mind about the other people involved in your example:**
>
> _____
>
> _____
>
> _____
>
> _____
>
> _____

Your objectives

Having these clearly in mind is the key, but surely they will be clear? Returning to the example of the company meeting, the objectives were, in effect, stated as being to ensure the event will be successful, felt by everyone to be an appropriate function; and a memorable one, something that sets the scene for a successful year to come. But it is not actually as straightforward as that. What about cost? Are those objectives regardless of cost? Or within a particular budget? Or equipment for visual aids? Here we again meet variables and the scale basis on which we should view them. So, the answer may not be regardless of cost, but not to a ridiculous budget either. Everying is in fact, negotiable. If visual aids are vital, we might even change the date to secure the larger meeting room where the equipment can be better accommodated and the overall effect will be more professional.

The task here is to prepare by identifying what the objectives are, what the priorities are, what the variables are and what attitude do we have to each – can we compromise on them or not and if so on which and by how much? This preparation must be realistic. We are not going to get our own way 100% on every detail.

The thinking here is important, and must include how you may need to *justify* through argument to show the advantage of your point of view, particularly on the points you want to win. It must also consider which variables you might use as *concessions*, that is, on which areas are you prepared to reduce your objectives if necessary and give something away, ideally to obtain something else in return.

Variables and their use.

As we will see, a major part of negotiation consists of *trading concessions*. A give and take process – '. . . if we start an hour later, and choose an alternative menu, can we have the larger room at the same costs? . . .' – that you will handle very much better if you are ready with some of the options.

Set clear objectives for your example:

_____

_____

_____

_____

_____

The structure

The final element of the way we prepare is structure – what we do first, second and third. It means how much time we anticipate spending, and also knowing in advance, which we will make prime and subsidiary points.

Structure in this sense seems obvious and deceptively simple. A good report has a beginning, a middle and an end. Likewise, a good speech and it balances content with humour, asides and digressions in a measured manner. As has been said of preparation, generally this does not just happen, it needs thinking through.

As we review the conduct of negotiation, the shape and detail within that shape will become progressively clearer.

Make some initial notes on the structure of the meeting in your example:

_____

_____

_____

_____

_____

Conduct

When negotiation takes place, two separate factors are in train and worth considering separately; first the process – the tactics of negotiation and secondly, the interpersonal behaviour which accompanies them.

How to manage the process effectively.

In this section, we start by reviewing the tactical basis for negotiation. Let us begin by returning to what we called 'variables' earlier. Variables are the key to negotiation. It has already been stated that we may have to give as well as take 'variables', a fact that means those which are traded are often referred to as 'concessions'. Some are concessions from them to us, some vice versa. Negotiation is, in fact, the process of trading concessions. Not that we intend to haggle about everything, the trick is to identify all the possible concessions, but then use them sparingly.

Using the variables.

A knowledge of all the variables and their possible use as concessions to be traded is key. We must know the variables in order to prepare an opening strategy – a starting point. We must know the variables so that we can use some appropriately to trade with. At the same time, we must continue to search for variables throughout the negotiation.

Few negotiating situations are a foregone conclusion. Occasionally, one party holds all the cards and the outcome is not in doubt. More often, the power is reasonably evenly spread between the parties. Power to sway the course of the negotiation is something both hope to bring to bear. A major mistake sometimes made is for the negotiator either to underestimate his own power or to over estimate that of the other party.

What gives you power in negotiation? Well, a number of things. Power comes from 'promise of reward' – you can provide something the other wants, so he has to listen. It comes also from the opposite – 'threat of punishments' is the apparent intention *not* to provide something the other party wants. But, there are other things too. Specific variables, which may be either tangible (like some of the things we noted about the refrigerator – capacity to hold bottles or the star rating of its freezer compartment); or intangible (like perhaps the fact that you are a regular customer, or Chairman of the local Chamber of Commerce). Power comes also from 'legitimacy', that is factual evidence, something clearly correct that weighs in the argument (like the same fridge clearly advertised in a sale along the road); and also from what are called 'bogeys', something fielded specifically to produce an edge – sympathy perhaps (' . . . with this leg in plaster, I can only buy where I can get delivery . . .').

111

A final power source worth noting is confidence. This, as has already been mentioned comes, in part, from preparation. More of this will be studied in the next chapter.

As you think through what the bargaining variables are, you should do so alongside an assessment of how much power they give you. More variables, whilst undeniably useful, do not automatically guarantee power by virtue of their sheer weight of numbers. A few telling ones may, in fact, be more useful.

Four negotiation commandments.

Four other principles are important to have in mind as you start the process.

First, **aim high**. 'Faint heart never wins fair lady' the saying has it. Similarly it is easier to aim for the top, for the best deal you can imagine, rather than start too low. You can always trade down. Indeed you may well have to, but it is more difficult to trade up – particularly at a late stage in the game.

Different kinds of variable.

With this in mind it may be worth, especially in complex negotiations with many variables, separating the variables into three priority categories:

- the **'musts'**: what we feel we must take from the negotiation if the deal is to be at all acceptable to us
- the **'ideals'**: what we intend to get, to make the ideal deal
- the **'loss leaders'**: what we are prepared to trade in order to agree a deal (even if we would prefer to keep them). Remember trading concessions are fundamental to the process, you must have some things in their category for negotiation to work.

If this thinking is clear in the mind as we start, the process will be easier. It will also make it more likely that we get off to a good start, important in itself, and also good for the confidence.

Secondly, **get the other person's shopping list**. We must not just concentrate on our own side but on the total situation – how much can we infer or anticipate about their likely position? The more accurate a picture we have, the better the position we will be in. This may come from prior preparation, knowledge and experience of the person or situation, or from questioning during initial conversation before negotiation as such begins.

Thirdly, **keep the whole package in mind**. That is your view and theirs together so that you proceed conscious of everything, or as much as possible, that will be involved.

And fourthly, **keep searching for variables**. Remain flexible. Nothing that has been written so far is meant to imply that knowledge, planning and so on should then act like a straight-jacket. The good negotiator is quick on his feet. Sometimes what happens is very much along the lines you expect, never exactly so, of course. Fine-tuning is always necessary. On other occasions all the best laid plans are to no avail and we must fall back on experience and native wit.

Now the process. Remember negotiation assumes a point of balance, that whilst participants start at opposite ends of the scale they will settle, finally, on something they can both relate to as a 'good deal'. This concept of a range of possibilities and a point of balance is important, and is illustrated in Figure 8.

The point of balance will not always be spot-on, a range of solutions are possible around the middle point. Similarly the furthest points from the centre are usually instantly recognised by both parties as unrealistic. Negotiation can thus be represented as the to and fro process that moves up and down the line and dictates where things finally settle.

Where we start is therefore very important. The starting point, for either party, is usually referred to as their **initial stance**. Judgement is necessary regarding the placing of the initial stance. At one end of the scale we can go for a **quick kill**:

The starting point: the initial stance.

> '*Here are our conditions – take them or leave them.*'

When we are in a powerful position this could be appropriate, or certainly something towards this end. But even if we are, it is important

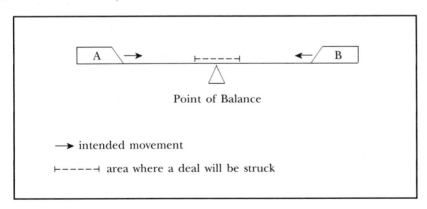

Point of Balance

→ intended movement

⊢-----⊣ area where a deal will be struck

Figure 8   The point of balance

to save face and for the ritual of negotiation to be seen to be done. Credibility is important too. If people are expecting some movement they may simply not believe that a hard initial stance will not be changed.

At the other end of the scale, we might start on a different note:

'Let's talk about what you want, we are reasonable people.'

This is more appropriate when we feel we may be at a disadvantage, but go too far with it and we will be.

The initial stance must be in mind, and will no doubt come early on but first we must review where we are so far. Negotiation rarely comes out of the blue. There is usually a history of contact between the two parties. This may be in writing, correspondence perhaps. Or a number of meetings, just one, or even a few words exchanged before we started negotiating. Whatever it is, it sets the scene. To an extent, it provides the agenda. And we do need an agenda in mind – something which recaps the history, and states the case so far and our initial stance – perhaps an exaggerated one which stresses the benefits (see Part One) and makes our case persuasive. Remember that persuasion precedes negotiation. In addition, we must recap any elements already agreed. Some negotiations are based on a preferred set of terms and conditions, the alteration of which can change the whole balance of the deal.

It is sometimes said that the higher the opening bid (initial stance), the better the final deal. It is difficult to negotiate down from nothing, and an initially exaggerated stance has the effect of pulling the other party off-balance, changing his perception of how and where a deal may be struck. See Figure 9.

This can even mean the first round of negotiation is only to shift to a more reasonable initial stance, then the bargaining can really start.

On the one hand, the taking of initial stances seems to distance the two parties, like two knights lining up on hill tops to each side of a valley. On the other hand, the way this is done, the totality of the exchange to this point needs to build what are called **'bridges of rapport'**. These are designed to bring us together and do so in a way that sets the scene for achieving what we want.

Building bridges to agreement.

The other party is more likely to see your points of view if he can relate to you, so bridges should make this more likely. A number of approaches can serve this purpose. They are, for example:

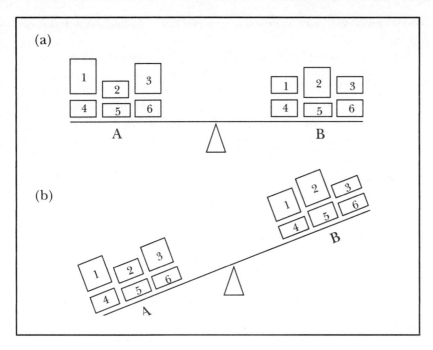

Figure 9   Changing perceptions of the variables as negotiation progresses

- open the discussion on a neutral subject to allay any hostility, and to obtain initial agreement and get the other person into a conversation
- when holding back, assure him you will make every effort to come to a mutually agreeable out-turn
- demonstrate respect for him and for the process. For example, compliment him on an action which has helped in the negotiation
- refer back to agreement. Reinforce your persuasion by linking to his needs and how he agreed you can help
- present values in your offering (even if some of them may later be negotiated out)
- try to present a clear explanation, justification if appropriate, for any complex issues to be dealt with.

All such tactics put the conversation on a basis of sweet reasonableness. So too does getting his shopping list. Interest in his side, his views, his needs can be put over as genuine concern but help find out what is on his list.

Keep finding out more.

So, ask questions; listen (really listen) to the answers and get him to spell out his position. Trading concessions may start at this stage, and can involve peripheral issues which nevertheless set the scene for what is to follow. Even at this stage, we should never give things away. Avoid saying 'why don't we talk this through over lunch; my treat'; instead say 'if you agree to come to an agreement today, I will buy us lunch and we can chat things through in comfort'. If this kind of swop is handled informally, then no one feels boxed in and the conversation can move naturally to a more business-like level.

Then the trading can really start. This can take the form of tentative exploration, starting as in the example above '. . . if . . . then . . .', or more specifically, even demanding in tone.

The golden rules of trading concessions.

There are two golden rules at this stage, and a number of ways of going about applying them. We will investigate both.

Rule One: 'Never give a concession. Trade it, reluctantly'.

The first part is important because the number of variables is finite and you want your share. The second because perception is as important to how things go as fact. We want to be *seen* to be driving a hard bargain.

Rule Two: 'Optimise or minimise every concession'.

Or, more specifically, optimise yours, and minimise his in terms both of value and the way we talk about it. In other words, build up the value, significance and importance of anything you offer and minimise that of what is offered to you. This is worth a few examples.

First *optimising your concessions* this means:

- stressing the cost (financial or otherwise) to you. ('Well, I could do that but it will involve me in a lot more work.')
- exaggerate – credibly. That is do not overstate and, if possible provide evidence. ('Well, I could do that but it will involve me in at least twice as much work. I have just been through . . .')
- refer to a major problem your making a concession will solve.

('Well, I suppose if I was to agree it would remove the need for you to . . .')

- imply it is an exceptional concession ('I would never normally do this, but . . .')
- imply it is not only exceptional but beyond the call of duty. ('I really don't know what my boss will say but . . .')

Additionally, with someone you have dealt with before:

- Refer to past discussions and the value of what you did for him then ('Remember how useful so-and-so was? Well, I suppose I could . . .')

Such lead-ins not only build the significance of what you are offering, and make it more likely to be accepted, but also make it more likely to be accepted quickly; because there is an implied urgency.

Secondly, **minimising their concessions**, even as you accept or agree to them, this means:

- do not overdo the thanks (not a profuse 'Thank you so much', but a brief – even dismissive 'thanks' – this is as much a matter of tone as of the phrase used)
- depreciate them, that is belittle the value ('Right, that's a small step forward, I guess')
- amortise them where appropriate. That is divide them where smaller units will sound less impressive ('Well, at least that saves me X every month – rather than quoting the total figure)
- treat them as given, not in fact of value (a brief acknowledgement may be all that is necessary here – 'Right, let's do it that way')
- take it for granted, in other words treat it as if it is no concession at all, rather a foregone conclusion ('Fine, I would certainly expect that')
- devalue by implying you have what is being offered already ('OK, though I have already . . .')
- accept, but imply you are doing a favour ('I don't really need that, but, fine let's arrange things that way if it helps')
- link value to time, implying it is now not worth what is implied ('Well, that helps a little, but is not of major importance now we have done . . .')
- deny any value ('That really doesn't help').

117

ACTION

Consider how you will deal with the variables in your example:

_____

_____

_____

_____

_____

As both these principles are deployed as the discussion progresses, the skilled negotiator is the person who trades a concession which in fact costs him little, but has an implied value which brings a relatively more valuable concession in return from the other side.

This is what gives us an edge. After all, a concession which we offer but state, or allow to be seen, as of little or no value is unlikely to prompt the offer of anything other than a low value concession in return. Thus, throughout the process we must play down our thanks for concessions gained because of what we describe as their low value, and build up the value of everything we concede. The only restraint on this exaggeration is the need to retain a suitable measure of credibility with the other person.

It is all a question of degree. People know there is a ritual to negotiation, they know a line is being taken but still have to form a judgement of how far.

With these two overall rules in mind, we will turn to some of the other techniques that can be used along the way. There are many, and more will be implied later when we review what is going on in terms of the interpersonal behaviour involved. For the moment let us review ten key techniques to keep things manageable, and demonstrate the process at work.

Ten Techniques that Help Keep You Ahead

1. **Use silence.** When you say nothing it may be as powerful as when you say something, provided it is used at the right time and in the right way. As most people quickly feel embarrassed by a

silence, it can sometimes need a conscious effort to hold it; but it can be worthwhile. For example:

- if we cannot optimise or minimise, silence can imply we are non-committal.
- a silence can imply certainty on our part (and prompt uncertainty in the other person). Thus having made a clear suggestion '. . . so what do you think?' We wait. Do not allow the pause to push you into diluting what you have just said unnecessarily.

2. **Summarise frequently.** Negotiations are, by definition, complex. They involve juggling a number of variables. It is easy to lose the thread, so never be afraid to summarise – where we have got to so far, how we left one aspect of the discussion. Linking this to using 'suppose' or 'if' keeps the conversation organised and allows us to explore possibilities without committing ourselves. ('Right, we have agreed that we need to sort cost, delivery and timing, now if . . . then . . .')

3. **Make notes.** As stated in (2) above, complex negotiations have to be kept track of throughout their course. Whilst the formality of certain meetings is insufficient for note-taking to be seen as appropriate, at most this can and should be done. Information is power. Never leave yourself groping – 'What did we say about so-and-so?' – Not only will taking notes prevent you being caught out on something factual which you cannot, for the moment, recall from earlier in the conversation, but making them or checking them can have another advantage. It gives you time to think. Either as you say 'let me make a note of that' (or are obviously doing so) or 'let me check what we agreed about that', you can be thinking. The brain works a good bit faster than the pen. It is sometimes surprising just how much thought you can bring to bear as you write two or three (sometimes irrelevant) words on your pad.

4. **Leave them feeling each step is good.** Negotiation tends to build up agreement progressively. Make sure you emphasise that each stage is good – preferably for both parties, but particularly for them – as we proceed. Phrases like 'that's a good

arrangement', 'that will work well', 'that's fair', 'that's a good suggestion, let's do it that way' help the agreement build.

5. **Read between the lines.** Remember it is essentially an adversarial process. Both parties want the best for themselves, and the only signs of approaching traps come via the other person, as do signs of success around the corner. Particularly watch for danger phrases, those which often mean something other than what they seem to mean. And can mean the opposite of what they say. For example:

'You're a reasonable fellow' (meaning 'I am')

'That's much fairer to us both' (meaning '. . . and especially fairer to me')

'It looks like we are almost there' (meaning '. . . there is something else I want')

'Now, we only need to clear up a couple of minor details' (minor? for whom?)

'That's everything' (followed by '. . . but, for one more thing . . .')

6. **Maintain neutrality** as much, and as long, as possible. Negotiation works best as a balancing exercise. If we throw the whole basis of discussion up in the air – '. . . it is not as good as the other deal I am considering' we are back to square one. We may want to go back, we may not be happy with the other offer, never mind the terms and conditions, but that is another process – back to persuasive communication.

7. **Keep thinking** – and build in time to think. The power of silence has already been mentioned. Use it to think ahead. Use any delaying tactic, working something out on a calculator, even making a telephone call, but do not let your mouth get ahead of your brain. Of course, if you can encourage the other person to do just that, so much the better.

8. **Keep your powder dry.** Try not to make an offer, certainly not a final offer, until everything that needs negotiating is out on the

table. This may need no more than a question. 'Yes, I am sure I can help there; is there anything else that you want to consider?' Or, if necessary, questions; keep pursuing the point.

9. **Do not get hung-up on deadlines.** There is an old saying that there has not been a deadline in history that was not negotiable. Time, timing, all aspects of it are always variables. How long will things take? When will they happen? All at once? Always keep this aspect in mind.

10. **Constraints and variables are interchangeable.** Almost anything the other side presents as fixed can be made into a variable. Fixed is as likely to mean not wanting to negotiate, as not able to be negotiated.

None of these are themselves complex, they illustrate very clearly the multifaceted nature of negotiation. There is a great deal going on. The trick is in the orchestration of what we are to do. It helps to be in the driving seat. Shakespeare in 'Much Ado About Nothing' put it well 'Two men ride of a horse, one must ride behind'.

Run the conversation *you* want, in a way that *they* find acceptable, professional if you will. Getting off to a good start sets the process in train, fine-tuning as you go along keeps you progressing matters as you want. And this (picking up point 5 above) means being extra conscious of what the other person appears to be up to, and of how the interpersonal behaviour of the transaction is likely to work. This is reviewed separately a little later.

To give a better feeling of just how some of the issues reviewed so far work, we turn to an example. The next section, mainly in the form of a conversation, shows something of the flow and sequence of the negotiation process as it must occur in a dynamic, interactive, manner.

◀ CHAPTER 9 ▶

NEGOTIATION IN ACTION

Deploying the Techniques

Negotiating is a practical art. It is one thing to dissect and discuss it, it is another to put it into practice. So, before summing up we will examine a case, looking at something of how it all works in practice. The following poses a simple situation – with just sufficient complexity for there to be something to negotiate. It is intended to reflect real life, but simplifies the issues somewhat (avoiding the detailed financial figures involved, for instance).

An example of the way the techniques are used.

The situation

Pat Owen runs a small business in public relations. She also writes articles, company material and books. Her small business is thriving, so much so that she has decided her now ancient and trusty typewriter must give way to a word processor. After some research, she has decided on suitable equipment and has asked a salesman from the office equipment company to visit her to discuss the quotation he has submitted.

John Burn works for Computing Clobber. He is an experienced salesman, he knows the equipment he sells and is keen to do a deal. Indeed, from his previous conversation with Pat Owen, he has inferred that she likes the package of equipment he has recommended, and he confidently expects to conclude the deal at the forthcoming meeting.

He arrives on time, and is offered and accepts a cup of coffee. Pat switches on the answer-phone to avoid interruptions and the discussions begin.

Before we eavesdrop on the discussion, we should bear in mind an overview of what each of them plans to achieve.

Pat has debated long and hard with herself about what she can afford. She wants something good, indeed it is very important to her. She wants the bigger (faster) of the two printers she has checked out. Above all, she would like to minimise the cost, yet as she has gone into the matter, there are additional items – extra software – that could be worth getting as well. The specification in the quote includes two packages.

Finally, a small point – she is worried about being away from her desk for the training that is necessary.

John believes he is close to an order, the equipment seems to be exactly what is wanted and he has offered a reasonable deal. He has some leeway on price (either in terms of reducing the price or juggling with the other elements) but wants a profitable sale. He sees it as the last part of the sales process rather than a negotiating one. He is mistaken and therefore not well-prepared.

Variables: You will find that various elements are used as variables during the conversation – the equipment itself, the software, delivery and installation, training, payment terms, the price and discounts, and even publicity.

Note: Ignore, for the moment, the numbers appearing in the text. These will be referred to later.

Now, to the conversation. With the initial pleasantries past, John turns to the business of the day.

J : You got our quote all right then?

P : Yes, thanks very much.

J : I hope you found it interesting.   *(He tests to discover her initial attitude.)*

123

P : Yes, indeed. I am not sure it is exactly right and I am comparing it with some others, but it was certainly clear. (1)

(She indicates that she is looking at other quotes and hints they are also good, or perhaps better.)

J : I see, in what way is ours not quite right?

(He attempts to clarify her last remark.)

P : Well, technically I am sure it is quite good. I am not a technical person (2), of course, but you seem to have reflected my brief well enough and I have no quibbles with that. However, I am after a total system; not just the w/p itself, but the software, printer and things like training as well. I think it's these areas we need to have a closer look at.

(She begins to soften up John.)

J : I see, perhaps you would tell me where you see any particular problem?

(He seeks further clarification.)

P : Well, I think there are several areas, perhaps we can take them one at a time. Let's deal with the ancillary equipment first. Now in your quote you recommend the faster of the two laser printers we discussed. As you know, I really want the faster printer rather than the more basic one if I can, and both a 3½ inch disk drive and a 5½ inch drive, so I can liaise with a colleague who has

*(P prefers to deal with one thing at a time and in the sequence of her choice. She starts with the other **equipment**.)*

124

material on that system. Now this will certainly do everything I want – a Rolls Royce job in fact but that printer does make the whole package more than I really hoped to spend (3). I am not sure that the second disk drive is essential. Anyway, I may well be able to manage without it. So what I suggest we do is that you let me have the 5½ inch drive on loan long enough to test it out.

(P indicates the total is too expensive.)

(P asks for a concession [trading something of low importance to her – the two drives].)

J : It is just the additional disk drive that you want on that basis?

(J clarifies.)

P : Yes, if I do want to keep it then it will postpone the payment for that element for just a while and means I can go for the better printer. See what I mean?

(always her intention)

J : Yes, I do.

P : It won't be difficult for you to arrange that (4) I am sure, and if I decide in favour, you will get payment for it anyway in, say, 6 months.

(P minimises the difficulty the point may make for him.)

J : Okay, I suppose I can arrange that – I'm pretty sure you will want to keep it anyway.

(J concedes what appears a small point.)

P : I expect you're right. Good, that's fine. Let's turn now to the question of software. I

*(P confirms the concession and turns to the second point: **software**. . .)*

would ideally like the graphics package and the one that will do my accounts as well as the full word processing. Would you be able to include those at no extra charge? They are not very costly but I must keep the overall cost down as I've said.

J : You didn't include those in the spec we quoted or did you?

(J begins to resist.)

P : No, I'm sorry – I hadn't been through all the literature at the time – but I can see they would be useful. It would make your overall arrangements much more attractive. (5)

(P apologises and repeats the request.)

J : It is an extra cost for us though . . .

(J continues to resist.)

P : Not very much in terms of the overall cost.

(P persist, minimising the effect.)

J : Well, perhaps not. I guess I could let you have those then if we go ahead.

(P agrees, reluctantly, to include the extra software.)

P : And you will deliver that along with everything else and include a run-down on them in the training?

(P adds on a request for a small, associated concession.)

J : Well I don't know, it will extend the training time and . . .

(J realises he has in fact given away more than he thought.)

P : But, they are not much good unless I can work them. I am sure I will pick it up fast and it won't extend the time to any real extent.

(The point is pressed, and the difficulty [time and cost] minimised.)

J : All right.

(He agrees.)

P : I appreciate that. Now, what next? Ah, yes the delivery and installation.

*(P raises third point: **delivery** and **installation** .)*

J : Well, that should be straightforward. Is that the last point?

(J attempts to get the rest of her shopping list.)

P : Yes. (6) Well apart from training but I am sure that's no problem, it's all included and you agreed to run me through the other software.

(P belittles what is described as the last point.)

J : Yes. – Okay. What about delivery? Here I suppose?

(Reassured, J goes back to the third point.)

P : That's right, I've got one of those units for it all to stand on ordered. Once I know which quote I accept, I can get that in first and away we go. Your people do install, don't they? I don't want a pile of boxes dumped on the doorstep.

J : Yes, of course, delivery and installation are all included.

P : And you will take away all the boxes and packing?

(P asks for a small extra.)

127

J : We don't usually do that. Can't you leave them for the dustman?

(J resists.)

P : The management company running this office complex is a bit strict about that sort of thing and their office is actually next door. In fact, he wants to come and see what equipment I get. If you can get all the boxes taken away, I can possibly recommend you. (7) I think he is thinking of a similar installation for his firm.

(P hints at future business prospects as a lever to obtain the concession.)

J : I'm still not sure that I can arrange that. Our despatch manager is very strict.

P : See what you can do, will you?

(This point is left hanging but P has a nice case to make to whoever delivers '. . . well, he said he'd fix it.')

J : Okay I will. Now what about training? If you decide to go ahead today, then I can get a date in the diary for you to visit the training centre.

(J tries to move ahead onto the last point – explains what needs to be done.)

P : And you think a day will be enough – even with the other software included?

(P checks details.)

J : Oh, yes, certainly. How about the week after next?

(J goes for agreement.)

P : Well, hang on – I was hoping you could get your trainer to

(P introduces another, expected, concession required.)

come here. Would that be
possible?

J : Well, it is certainly possible, but *(J is determined to give*
there would be an extra cost. *nothing away.)*

P : You remember I mentioned
earlier the other quotes I have?
(8)

J : Yes.

P : Well, one of the differences is *(P makes him feel*
that they are both willing to do *uncompetitive [just at a stage*
the training here. It means I *when he believes everything*
don't have to leave my phone *was agreed] and minimises the*
unattended. That's important *problem.)*
to someone working on her
own, you know. If we schedule
the date well ahead, it would
minimise the inconvenience.

J : Even so, we have a clear scale *(J resists.)*
of charges for in-house visits
and with what I have already
agreed . . .

P : Well, I see the problem but it *(P emphasises the prospect of*
would be a pity to fall out at *the order.)*
this stage. Everything else seems
fine. May I make a suggestion?

J : What exactly? *(J tries to clarify.)*

P : I have been asked by one of the
office equipment journals (she
names a well-known one) to
write a feature on the writer's
use of word processors. If I buy
yours, I shall have to use it as

129

an example - after all it will be
the only one I've got! If I
promise to mention your firm
by name, do you think your
boss would agree to the training
being done here? It would be
such a help. At least ask him.
He might like the idea. (9)

*(P makes the request seem to
have clear compensations – she
sells it.)*

J : I can certainly ask, it sounds a
good swop to me. Will you
leave it with me?

(J conditionally agrees.)

P : Yes, of course - see what
reaction you get.

J : Right. So we seem to be
agreed. We let you have the
second drive on 6 months' loan,
include the additional software,
and I will work on the training
being done here.

P : And on getting all the boxes
cleared away - yes?

J : That's right, nearly forgot. Now
- can we go ahead on that
basis?

(J tries to wrap up the deal.)

P : Yes, . . . I think we can . . . but
there is just one small thing.
Again this is included in the
other quotes, and that's
insurance.

(P raises an extra area.)

J : What do you mean?

(J queries.)

P : They offer a free year's insurance as part of the package.

J : On the same machine and costing?

P : Not exactly, I suppose, but similar.

(P concedes it is not like for like.)

J : You have to look at the other deal you know. With the price we have quoted and the extras, there is no possibility of my matching that.

(J refuses.)

P : Well, I suppose I have to accept that. Even so it is a bit of a disappointment. Your company offers the best arrangements in many ways, but even with the items we have agreed it is still not the most competitive. I take it you do want the business?

(P suggests how reasonable she is . . .)

(. . . raises a price objection.)

J : Yes, indeed we do.

P : Perhaps you would consider adjusting the overall discount to make up for my having to fix and pay for insurance separately?

(. . . and makes a suggestion.)

J : I believe our original price was very keen, and we do, as I said, want the order. But I don't really have any more leeway over the discount.

(J resists.)

P : I'm sure your price is keen, but as I said it is not the most competitive.

(P puts his quote on the spot by reminding him of the competitors.)

J : Well, what sort of difference are we talking about?

P : To really make everything we have said add up to the best deal all round. I suppose the discount would need to go up by $7\frac{1}{2}\%$ or so.

J : That's a lot of money. The margins on this kind of system are not so great.

(J resists.)

P : How far can you go?

(P squeezes.)

J : Myself? Well, I think with what we have already agreed, I cannot go beyond 4% at this stage. That will be my limit.

P : And how far can your company go at the next stage? (10)

*(P presses to test that the overall limit is **really** being reached.)*

J : 'At this stage' is just a turn of phrase. 4% will be the company's limit.

P : No good me calling your boss, you mean?

(P questions J's status and authority.)

J : No, I'm afraid not.

P : But you can go to 4% more discount?

J : Yes, I can.

 P : I hoped you would go to 7½%   *(P belittles the offer.)*
to match the others completely,
but let's see what we have
agreed. You will lend me the   *(throws in **current** price)*
5½" drive and invoice after 6
months at the current price,
you will include the other
software and find out about the
training – and the boxes – and
reduce the price by another 4%.

 J : Yes, that's it.

 P : On that basis, I think we have   *(P closes the discussion and the*
a deal. Would you like another   *deal.)*
coffee while we tie up the
paperwork?

It took a little while, there are still loose ends but the deal has improved markedly. It may be that Pat is depicted as doing too well (though margins on such products are high and the salesman has still, no doubt, obtained a profitable deal) – but she handled it well and deserved to win the majority of points. She certainly did better than others, approaching the same process less well prepared might have done.

The right-hand column of commentary makes clear her tactics.

The 'score': to summarise the outcome, John gets his order, of course, but Pat wins on a number of concessions:

- 6 months' loan of the 5½" disk drive (and later) payment for it, after 6 months at current price
- 2 additional, free, pieces of software
- the boxes and packing taken away on delivery – perhaps
- training at her office, rather than at the training centre – probably (though she could have opted to make her order conditional)
- a 4% additional discount.

She has not managed to get free insurance, and has offered

collaboration on an article, and tacitly promised a recommendation to a colleague.

She has saved enough to finance the printer she really wanted and still come out ahead. But she led the process. She worked through systematically, she was prepared, she negotiated.

John on the other hand, emerges sadder but wiser; at least let us hope so. He has the order, it may even be reasonably profitable, but he is no doubt saying to himself '. . . if only . . .' and that we should aim to avoid.

Reading between the lines.

Ten hidden meanings

All negotiation will tend to have a 'subtext' of hidden meanings. Some disguising the true feeling, some there to draw attention the fact all is not quite as it seems.

The numbers in the preceding text indicate some examples of this, and below are related to possible meanings. (You may want to look at the text of the conversation again as you look now at this list.)

From text	*Possible meaning*
1. '. . . it was certainly clear.'	but not exactly right
2. 'I am not a technical person . . .'	You can handle me easily
3. '. . . does make the whole package more than I really hoped to spend . . .'	I may not buy unless I get a better deal
4. 'It won't be difficult for you . . .'	a little flattery . . .
5. '. . . make your overall arrangements much more attractive.'	without it, it is less (or not attractive)
6. 'Yes.'	for the moment
7. '. . . I can possibly . . .'	nothing promised, no degree of likelihood

8. 'remember . . . the other quotes'	I am not decided yet. Don't lose it at this stage.
9. '. . . he might like the idea.'	and thank you for it
10. '. . . at the next stage'	can anyone else in your organisation decide differently from you?

CHAPTER 10

INTERPERSONAL BEHAVIOUR

It's Not What You Do, It is the Way That You Do It

Techniques can only work if you utilize the people and their behaviour.

Negotiation is not simply a matter of technique, though this is important. It is also dependent on 'reading' the other people involved. To a degree of course, this is a factor of experience and that in turn, needs time to accumulate. Nevertheless certain principles can be useful, both immediately and to help genuine experience build up quickly. (You know the old saying that you can have five years' experience or one year's experience multiplied by five; the latter, of course, being better.)

This section looks at key behavioural aspects – listening, questioniong, and non-verbal signals (body language) – but starts by reviewing some of what goes on, as it were, 'between the lines'.

Verbal signs

Negotiation has a language of its own. Some of it becomes ritual, it adds nothing to persuasiveness. It may be so 'over the top' as to be clearly part of the fabric rather than the content of what is being said. Some is a ploy, and we need to read between the lines to see what motivation lies behind the comment or phrase.

For example, consider the hidden signals in the following:

One party says:

- 'We would find it extremely difficult to meet the deadline.'

and means:

'If we do meet it, it must be worth something.'

- 'Our organisation is not set up to cope with that.' 'So, if we do, consider it a real favour.'

- 'I do not have the authority to arrange . . .' '. . . but someone else does.'

- 'It is not our normal practice to do that.' 'I could make an exception.'

- 'I never negotiate on price.' 'If you want to – you start.'

- 'We can discuss that point.' 'It is negotiable.'

- 'We are not prepared to discuss that at this stage.' 'But we will later.'

- 'That's very much more than our budget.' 'So, it better offer real value and extra benefit.'

- 'It is not our policy to give additional discounts and if we do they will not be as much as 10%.' 'Would you accept 5%?'

- 'Our price for that quantity is X.' 'But, for a larger quantity . . .'

- 'That's the standard terms and conditions.' '– but, we can negotiate.'

- 'It seems an extremely reasonable arrangement.' 'It is best for me.'

- 'It is a good price.' 'It is profitable for us.'

- 'I can't say I am happy with the arrangement but . . . 'I agree, but may ask for something else.'

And so on, and so on. You can probably think of, and will no doubt spot in future, many more. The detail, the nuances, of everything said when negotiating is very important. Does it mean what it seems? Can we check? Is it a ploy?

It is wise to be constantly watchful, to take nothing at face value and to consider numbers of factors, remembering that when you use them they help you. If you see the other party using them then they may be warning signs, and potentially put you at a disadvantage. Recognising them, and their potential danger, is the first step to overcoming them if they are deployed against us.

A number of such factors are now reviewed, in turn:

Keep the temperature under control

A considered approach works best.

We negotiate best when pursuing a calm, considered approach. So does the other person. Whilst we do not want to make it easy for them, quite the reverse, we do not want the fabric of negotiation to collapse either. Any behaviour we use must help our cause without, as it were, demolishing the table we sit at.

It is easy to get into a position where apparently pursuing our cause does more harm than good. For instance, if you labour on an issue on which agreement is clearly difficult, particularly early on in a discussion, to the point where you dig your heels in and refuse to budge, then you may create an overall impasse from which it is difficult for either party to retreat. You need to keep the range of issues in mind. If necessary, leave one point on one side to return to later. Having agreed some of the issues, overall views change. With an overall deal now in prospect, the early sticking point may not seem so important and can be dealt with without real difficulty.

Hidden motives

What goes on 'under the surface'.

Icebergs are a danger to shipping not so much because of what can be seen of them, but because of what can not. Nine-tenths of their bulk is hidden under the water. The iceberg concept can apply to negotiation. You say something, ask something perhaps, and do not seem to get a straight answer. Suspicion by the other party may prevent that straight answer. They are so busy looking for hidden motives that they hinder agreement for no good reason. It makes sense to spell out *why* you are doing things, asking a certain question, pursuing a certain line; so that at least most of what is hidden becomes clear. Of course, you may have motives you *want* hidden, at least for the moment, and that is fine. But if the other person thinks you are being several times more devious than you are, this will not help matters.

'Flagging'

Prompt thought not simply retaliation.

Clear 'flagging' of how you are proceeding can help therefore. Sometimes it just makes clear what you are doing –

- 'May I ask . . .?' or 'Perhaps, I might suggest . . .?'
at other times a specific reason
- 'I think it might . . . first . . .'
making getting . . . what we want more likely. It is seen as a constructive
step forward.

On the other hand, the one thing we should never flag is disagreement. This is something to watch as the natural, human, response, is to
flag it instantly. Consider what happens in a simple example. *A* makes
a suggestion – 'Perhaps we can aim for completion of stage one by
Friday week.' *B* immediately disagrees – 'No, I think that's far too long.'
Even if he goes on to explain why, and even if he is right, *A* is busy
developing a retaliatory response from the moment he hears the word
'No'. He does not listen to the explanation of why, and even if he half
hears it, is already committed in his own mind to his riposte. What is the
answer to this dilemma? People are more likely to listen constructively
and accept reasons given if they are given before disagreement is flagged.
Thus, if *A* makes his point, *B* might respond along the lines of 'That
would be ideal, however we agreed that the whole project should be
finished by the end of the month. Does Friday week leave sufficient time
for everything else?' There is much more chance that this will prompt
thought, discussion and that a compromise can be found, or a counter
suggestion accepted.

Summarise
Good negotiators summarise regularly. After all many negotiations can
get quite complex and discussions can last a while. Summarising can test
progress and allow us to rephrase in our own words things said by the
other party. It can help gain the initiative or lead in the discussion or
maintain the dialogue, and generally ensure similar interpretations and
avoid misunderstanding and subsequent acrimony.

Keep the record straight.

Psychological attack
Some things are said, not as themselves part of any argument but to put
the other party at a psychological disadvantage – to rattle them. Some
may be based on issues which are part of the discussion, such as pressure
put on timing and deadlines. Others may be solely 'cosmetic', like the
elaborate lighting of a pipe to create a long silence (during which they
are thinking and you are sweating). All sorts of things can be used in this
way, amongst them:

Something to put the other person off balance.

- playing for time (working something out on a calculator or making a phone call)
- a smoke screen of demands (only one of which is important)
- flattery or coercion
- an angry outburst or show of emotion
- (apparent) total fluency with the facts (wondrous mental arithmetic may have been worked out beforehand, or just be a guess which sounds authoritative)
- physical arrangements (an uncomfortable chair or position, balancing a coffee cup and trying to take notes)
- financial restraints made to seem irreversible
- pretended misunderstanding.

Defend/attack spirals

If you must attack, do so without warning.

Because people feel it is not proper to hit someone without warning, disagreement often starts from mild beginnings. Whilst one party says, 'I am not sure about this', and 'I think we should aim for better than that', gently moving towards a major negative, the other senses what is happening and begins to prepare a counter argument.

Good negotiators do not put the other party on their guard, if it is appropriate to attack they do so without warning.

Counter proposals

Avoid monologues.

Suppose you make proposal X and then the other person makes proposal Y. If you automatically think they are disagreeing, you will not be receptive and may not consider the alternative properly. If so, your riposte can lead into a series of monologues, with both sides seeing the other as unhelpful and unconstructive. Progress is blocked when, if X and Y are not so far apart, things could be moving together.

The deadlock

Keep the give and take going.

The purpose of negotiation is to make a deal. Deadlock does nothing for either party. The search for variables has to go on – and, if necessary, on – until a deal is possible. It is usually only a question of time. However, if there are moments of deadlock, it is helpful to think of the conversation flowing like a stream, which will always find a path round obstructions rather than through them.

Never underestimate the chances of a new path (nor overestimate your opponent's power and determination to remain unmoving). If you try to find out *why* there is a deadlock, and search widely for concessions or variables that will break the deadlock, it can usually be done. In dire cases, suggest a break (agree as much as possible before it) or even the involvement of other people.

The ritual game of negotiation

In the East, of course, it is necessary to bargain in the shops and markets, not simply to secure a good price for whatever you are buying but to win respect. The process itself is important, not just the outcome. This is true of any negotiating situation. Thus some 'professional' negotiators, who enjoy the game, feel frustrated if agreement is too quick or too simple. Negotiation must be allowed to take its course, and they will put up more and more conditions or elements to keep the process going.

Allow the other person's expectations of how things will proceed.

In such circumstances, it may be wise never to make the first offer, not to make unacceptable conditions or drive impossible bargains. And above all, give it time. I remember buying a watch on my first visit to the East, in Hong Kong, some 15 years ago. I had been told about the bargaining, and the percentage drop in price for which I should aim. I set off round the shops and, despite my best efforts, I could get only half way towards the suggested discount. Back at the hotel, discussing this with a local colleague, I asked what I was doing wrong. 'How long were you in each shop?' he asked. Replying that it was 10 minutes or so, he suggested I tried again and gave it half an hour. I then discovered that only after twenty minutes or so, when you were sitting on a stool and coffee had been produced did the bargaining get serious. This time I came out with a nice watch and a good deal – and more knowledge about the psychology of negotiation. There are limits of course, but if the other party wants to take his time it may be worth it in the end. Timing is an important factor, and has to be handled just right.

Future relationships

Always aim to end on a pleasant note. Negotiation can get acrimonious, hard bargains are driven, but people need to work or play together again. It may be good for future relations for the last move to be towards the other party, maybe throwing in one last (small) 'sweetener' as the final agreement is made. This can stand you in good stead next time round, at any subsequent encounter, and with colleagues, of course, these may well be a regular part of your work.

End on a basis from which you can work in future.

Listening

**Always, always
listen to *everything*
the other person
says.**

You have no doubt noticed that many problems of communication are
due to people not listening. Pardon? Read that last sentence again.
Listening is always important, and in a complex interaction such as
negotiation, it is especially important.

It does not just happen. It is easy to be distracted, and you need to
concentrate. Give the other party your full and undivided attention.
Another distraction is emotional. As the other person's argument
unfolds, you perhaps begin to feel anxiety or become angry in your
disagreement. If such resentment takes over and prevents you from
listening, your case will suffer. You will never combat an argument if
you only hear half of it.

In addition, never be afraid to interrupt a long speech to double check
you are following it. Ask for simplification or repetition if you wish.
Beware too of hearing what you want to hear. Do not make
assumptions, act on what the true message is.

You may need to analyse the message as it proceeds and begin to form
up a response, but you have to keep listening as you do so if you are not
to run into problems. You may well want to keep your first reactions
hidden. It can be difficult to come back saying that something is 'a
minor difficulty' if when it was raised your face registered total dismay.

Finally, think about what will make listening easier. You cannot
concentrate on what is being said if there is a lot of noise (for example,
an open-plan office, or children playing in the background), or if you are
busy with something else as you talk (in a car picking your way onto a
main road at a busy junction). Try to pick a time when you are at your
best, not over-tired or distracted by some personal emergency.

Remember if you pick up 100% of the message, you will be in a much
better position to respond effectively.

Questioning

**Do not proceed
without sufficient
information to
guide you.**

Always ask sufficient questions to help you with the whole process –
about the other person, their situation, their needs, their priorities. Open
questions, those which cannot be answered simply 'Yes' or 'No' and
tend therefore to start with what, where, why, how, who, are usually
best. They get people talking and will produce more information, which
in turn is the raw material for your case. It is difficult to find a black cat
in a dark coal cellar, perhaps until it scratches you. Similarly, it is
difficult to negotiate if there are too many gaps in your knowledge about
the situation. You will just find yourself in a corner.

142

Body language

We have looked at reading between the lines of what is said but the words (and tone, emphasis and so on) is not the only message which comes over when we speak with someone.

People project all sorts of non-verbal clues to their inner feelings. Whilst body language is an inexact science, it is certainly an interesting one and worthy of some study (the book, *Body Language – How to Read Others' Thoughts by their Gestures*, by Allan Pease (Sheldon Press) makes a useful reference).

So, whilst one gesture is not an infallible sign of anything (an unbuttoned jacket may only mean it is a tight fit! – wearing a jacket at all may mean fierce air-conditioning rather than formality) the checklist that follows is intended to provide some guidelines regarding what *may* be indicated by certain gestures.

Visual signs – interpret with care.

Body language clues

Open-mindedness shown by:
- Open hands
- Unbuttoned coat

Wariness shown by:
- Arms crossed on chest
- Legs over chair arm while seated
- Sitting in armless chair reversed
- Crossing legs
- Fistlike gestures
- Pointing index finger
- Karate chops

Thinking/analysing shown by:
- Hand to face gestures
- Head tilted
- Stroking chin
- Peering over glasses
- Taking off glasses – cleaning
- Glasses earpiece in mouth
- Pipe smoker gestures
- Getting up from table – walking

- Putting hand to bridge of nose

Confidence shown by:
- Steepling of the hands
- Hands on back of head – authority position
- Back stiffened
- Hands in coat pockets, with thumbs outside
- Hand on lapels of coat

Territorial Dominance shown by:
- Feet on desk
- Feet on chair
- Leaning against/touching object
- Placing object in a desired space
- Hands behind head – leaning back

Nervousness shown by:
- Clearing of throat

143

- Whew sound
- Whistling
- Cigarette smoking
- Picking-pinching flesh
- Fidgeting in chair
- Hands covering mouth while speaking
- Not looking at the other person
- Tugging at trousers or skirt while seated
- Jingling money in pockets
- Tugging at ear
- Perspiration/wringing of hands

Frustration shown by:
- Short breaths
- Tutting sound
- Tightly clenched hands
- Wringing hands
- Fistlike gestures
- Pointing index finger
- Running hand through hair
- Rubbing back of neck

Boredom shown by:
- Doodling
- Drumming fingers
- Legs crossed – foot kicking
- Head in palms of hands
- Blank stare

Acceptance shown by:
- Hand to chest

- Open arms and hands
- Touching gestures
- Moving closer to another
- Preening

Expectancy shown by:
- Rubbing palms
- Jingling money
- Crossed fingers
- Moving closer

Suspicion shown by:
- Not looking at you
- Arms crossed
- Moving away from you
- Silhouette body towards you
- Sideways glance
- Touch/rub nose
- Rubbing eye(s)
- Buttoning coat
- Drawing away

Alertness/Attention shown by:
- Hands on hips
- Hands on mid-thigh when seated
- Sitting on edge of chair
- Arms spread, gipping edge of table/desk
- Moving closer
- Open hands
- Hand to face gestures
- Unbuttoning coat
- Tilted head

Body language is something to keep an eye on through the whole process of negotiation, though it is only providing clues, a few pieces of the jigsaw, perhaps, and should not become a fixation. After all there are many other things to concentrate on.

Whatever is going on, the reason for being sensitive to what is said, the nuances, the gestures, everything that we do next must be based on two factors. The first commented upon earlier, is our plan; and the second is our reading of how things are going and how what has been done so far is being received. Negotiation demands constant 'fine-tuning'.

'Fine-tuning'

Just as in a sailing boat, a hand needs to be kept constantly on the tiller, to compensate for wind, tide and maintain smooth progress towards a destination, so it is with negotiation. In others words, however well-planned your tactics are, you are constantly having to respond to the other party. Sometimes this means dealing with something you expected, at least at some point and in some form. On other occasions it means responding quickly to things that are less expected or a complete surprise.

Direct the conversation throughout.

The overall objective is, of course, to remain on course to your objectives whatever happens, though there may well need to be some give and take. It is important that any response you make is, whilst it needs to be prompt, also considered. Some of this can only come with practice (and it is always worth some analysis afterwards to see what went well, less well and what there is to learn from it – whatever the outcome).

The following may help accelerate experience by indicating some of the tactics you may find yourself facing and suggesting both what the other party hopes for as a result, and the line of a possible response.

Line of behaviour taken by other party:	*Hoping you will:*
• **Chaos** – displays anger; storms out; takes umbrage	apologise, give concession, or get angry yourself, apologise, give concession

Action: Keep calm, express your concern at any misunderstanding, seek clarification, let things return to normal before trying to proceed.

• **Poor me** – plea for special sympathy, concern or approach because of their situation	give more because you feel sorry for them

Action: Do not be put off or (overly) sympathetic, acknowledge the problem, restate your position and take the conversation back on track.

Line of behaviour taken by other party: *Hoping you will:*

- **Not me** – claims they cannot make decisions; must refer to boss, spouse, committee or whatever

  this may be intended to exert pressure without souring relations ('it is not my fault')

  Action: Ask questions designed to ascertain whether what is said is true or just a ploy. (In some meetings, it may be an aspect worth checking early on – 'do you have the authority to make an arrangement or should we involve anyone else?')

- **Only option** – Keeps suggesting unacceptable option, without alternative

  be forced into agreement, seeing no option

  Action: Keep calm. Bear your objectives firmly in mind. Suggest other alternatives – middle ground, perhaps. Keep setting out the problem with their suggestions.

- **No way** – immediately stating one element as non-negotiable

  give up or offer a great deal to try to make it negotiable

  Action: Offer to set that element aside, moving on to other things and getting back to it once rapport is established and agreement is clear on some other elements.

- **What?** – over-reaction to something (shock-horror) to indicate impasse

  offer a rapid concession to compensate

  Action: Ignore the first response and restate the issue to prompt a more considered, informative response.

- **Can't** – opens with a problem – 'of course, we can't do anything unless the project can be completed by the end of the month'

  concede

  Action: Question for truth (it is more likely an initial stance), refer to the other variables.

Line of behaviour taken by other party: *Hoping you will:*

- **No-can-do** – a comment which contains no detail/reason but is very negative ('That's just not at all acceptable')

  see it as intractable and give in

Action: Ask for detail – *why* is it unacceptable? how different does it need to be? – Get away from the unspecific and down to the facts of the argument.

- **Something more** – an out-and-out request for some extra benefit.

  give it to gain goodwill and keep things going

Action: Investigate the trading possibilities. 'If I give you X, would you be able to agree to Y?'

- **Policy** – the 'rules' are quoted ('more than my job's worth') e.g. company policy

  read it as unchangeable and not even try to negotiate

Action: Check whether it is true, whether there are exceptions, whether others have authority to make exceptions. Rules are made to be broken but be prepared for this to be difficult on occasions, and, if necessary, be prepared to leave it.

- **Sell me** – negotiation is dependent on a tacit agreement (e.g. to buy, to action). If the deal is put in question, the whole situation may be changing

  give in to secure agreement

Action: Ask questions – do we go back to the stage of persuasion, or is it a ploy? If so, stick to your position and push back hard.

- **Big vs little** – a big deal is made of a small point, then used as a concession for something they really want

  see the first as a real issue and trade, in a way that is not a good exchange

Action: Check real importance, compare and deal with the two things together.

Line of behaviour taken by other party: *Hoping you will:*

- **No progress** – things appear   give in as the only way forward
  to be deadlocked, no clear way
  out

  <u>Action</u>: Suggest a real change – a break – an arbitrator. If it is a ploy,
  these may be resisted and you can get back on track.

If you are a regular negotiator, it may well be worth keeping notes of
your own more specific examples, as an *aide-memoire* for the future.

Overall, there are several aspects to negotiation. The process itself is
important, the structure and sequence of events contribute to its success.
The ritual may be important, the techniques certainly are, but it is
people that make it work. So no aspect of the inter-personal behaviour
involved must be overlooked. Any difficulty is less because the
individual elements are themselves complex, it is more in orchestrating
the whole. Those who get the whole moving effectively together, in
parallel, are likely to make the best negotiators.

Note a complete plan for your example:

1 *What* you plan to do:

_____

_____

_____

_____

_____

2 *How* you plan to go about it:

_____

_____

_____

_____

_____

3 **The other person's anticipated response and how you plan to deal with it:**

_____

_____

_____

_____

_____

◀ CHAPTER 11 ▶

SUMMARY

Two Checklists

Negotiation is perhaps well described as 'part art, part science'. Going about it in the right way increases the likelihood of success. However, it does not guarantee it. It is a dynamic, interactive process and needs to be conducted in a way that is well planned, yet flexible; that recognises that the people element is the most important – and the least predictable.

We have now reviewed something about the whole process – what it is, how it works, the techniques and interpersonal behaviour that are at the heart of it. To a degree, as has been said, it is a complex process. The danger of dissecting any such process, as is necessary to review it, is that it is difficult to put the pieces together. The section 'Negotiation in Action' and the conversation within it is intended to assist this process. Now, in summary, and in checklist form, we must attempt to pull together the essentials.

This is followed by a brief concluding section.

The checklist summary is in two parts. First, the principles; secondly, the tactics.

Checklist one: the principles

Principles of Negotiation:	*Implications:*
1. Definition: negotiation is about bargaining to reach a mutually agreeable outcome	This is the 'win-win' concept referred to earlier.

Principles of Negotiation:	*Implications:*
2. Never neglect your preparation	Have a clear plan (but remain flexible).
3. Participants must regard each other as equals	Mutual respect is essential to both conduct and outcome.
4. There is a need to 'abide by the rules'	Negotition is about discussion, rather than debate. There is little place for overt one upmanship or domination, yet each must 'fight his corner'.
5. Put your cards on the table	At least on major issues, i.e. do not pretend powers or state intentions that are simply untrue.
6. Patience is a key characteristic of the good negotiator	Take your time, do not rush discussion or decision-making. Delay is better than a poor outcome.
7. Empathy is vital	Put yourself in the other's shoes, see things from his point of view and do so objectively.
8. State clear objectives	Being open, early on, about overall intentions can save 'groping in the dark'.
9. Avoid confrontation	Do not get into a corner you cannot get out of. Avoid rows and showdowns, but stand firm and keep calm.
10. Position disagreement carefully	Act as devil's advocate, apparently looking at the case from the other's viewpoint, to avoid a confrontational 'I disagree' style.

Principles of Negotiation:	*Implications:*
11. Deal with concessions progressively	Where concessions have to be made, make them unwillingly, and one at a time – and trade them.
12. Do not let perfection be the enemy of the good	A 100% ideal outturn is rarely (if ever) an option. Be realistic and do not waste time and effort seeking something out of reach.
13. Use openness but not comprehensively	Declaring your plans, intentions may be useful to the discussion; the motivation behind them, why you have certain intentions or priorities you may want to keep hidden.
14. Stick with your objectives	Aim high, and settle as high as possible. Know when to drop the whole thing rather than agree to a totally inappropriate deal.
15. Keep up your guard	Maintain your stamina, bide your time. The other party may persevere for hours to see when you will crack.
16. Remain 'professional'	For example, respecting confidences that are given in the course of negotiations. Such consideration builds relationships and may help you next time.
17. Never underestimate people	A velvet glove may be disguising an iron fist.
18. End positively	Neither party will get exactly what they want, but if the deal is agreeable, emphasise this agreement at the end.

Checklist two: the tactics

Tactics of Negotiation:	*Implications:*
1. Select the right starting point	Your plan should make it easy for you to take the initiative and get quickly onto your agenda.
2. Aim high	Then the trading moves you less far from what you regard as a good position.
3. Do not make your feelings obvious	There is an element of bluff, if your face (and body language) say 'this is minor' as you tackle something major.
4. Use silence	Some things demand no reaction at all.
5. Watch for early difficulty	Let a rapport and momentum build up before you tackle contentious issues.
6. Do not exaggerate facts	These can be verified (or not) and cause problems later.
7. Communicate clearly	Remember (in the Introduction) the need for understanding as a foundation to the whole process.
8. Be seen to go with the other person's way of doing things	At least to some degree, and particularly if you are on 'their ground'.
9. Do not push too hard	There is usually a line beyond which the outcome is not a better deal, but complete breakdown.

153

Tactics of Negotiation:	*Implications:*
10. When negotiation is finished, stop	Once agreement is reached, clear, agreed (and perhaps noted) move on to other matters – so that you do not find people saying 'You know I have been thinking. . . .' and we are back to square one.

It will help you if you note these, and any other factors that *you* regard as key. After all, the importance of different factors does depend on the nature of the negotiation. Something full of complex financial details poses different problems from something simpler.

Finally, a few negative factors. **Do not:**

- over-react if reactions are negative as things proceed (after all the other person is at pains *not* to say how excellent every point is)
- allow yourself to become over-emotional, unpleasant, provocative, insulting (whatever the temptation). A display of emotion may be useful, but you must know what you are doing
- agree to something you do not want. In many situations, there is a minimal deal – below this it is better to walk away (your plan should identify this, if appropriate)

Every negotiating situation will teach you something – what works well, what to avoid. Remember, the detail is important. Sometimes what makes the difference between success and failure is something seeming small. One phrase, even one gesture may make the difference. If all the details are right, the whole will be more likely to work well.

◄ CHAPTER 12 ►

AFTERWORD

What Next?

So, there it is. A degree of persuasion must, needs be, form a part of what you do in communication if that communication is to be effective. The question should not be *should* you be persuasive, nor even *can* you be persuasive. There will be occasions when you do need to be persuasive and, as this book has hopefully demonstrated, you certainly can be – provided you bear certain techniques in mind and go about it in the right way. The question is *how*, exactly, can you deploy a persuasive argument in the right way on each occasion, so that you achieve your aims and yet whoever you are dealing with sees your approach as reasonable and finds it acceptable. This is the essence of both persuasive communication and negotiation.

There is no magic formula, so you will not win them all. But, if you work at it, and if, above all, you are conscious of what you wish to achieve and deploy a carefully chosen way for each meeting, each memo, each person as the need arises, you will win more and lose less.

There may be no one right way, but with a secure foundation of basic theory and psychology to work from, you will evolve a way that suits you. You will be respected by those with whom you deal and this will give you a good success rate of communications that work.

You may remember, a few years ago, Budweiser beer used an old story to illustrate one of their television advertisements. It showed a young lady, intent on a career in show business, saving the fare and flying to New York. She checks into a small hotel and, the following morning, sets out to find the great Mecca and American entertainment. Coming out onto the street, she asks a passerby, 'Tell me please, how do I get to Carnegie Hall?' He looks her straight in the eye and answers, 'Practise. You gotta practise.'

And this is no bad note on which to end a review of persuasive communication. You must practise. That sounds easy enough; but how exactly?

The key thing is to make a start and make sure that as you go on, the experience you gain helps make what you do in future better and better. Any skill seems a bit daunting at first. Remember the time when you learnt to drive? You went through a stage when you despaired of ever getting it together. Most people do; at least with driving. Communication and negotiation are no different. A basic 'shopping list' of techniques will start you off, allow you to practise and with the basic techniques in mind, you can add to your method of approach and continue to develop ad infinitum.

Final thoughts on what makes success more certain.

A few things are worth emphasising about this process of developing such skills. **First, preparation is key.** It really does make a significant difference. Yet it is so easy to miss out, or skimp. Make time for it, think about it, and everything else that follows will be easier.

Secondly, try and develop a consciousness of the communication and negotiation process. If your mind is actively aware of the overall issues, complexities and structure of what is involved, rather than simply moving from point to point, again the whole process will be easier. This will perhaps seem difficult to begin with. However, it is important. It does work and becomes easier with practice. In time, it will become a habit.

Thirdly, remember that confidence is paramount. Planning is the starting point for this, but if you have thought about both the principles, and the detail of a particular encounter, you will be more confident. This will not only help you, it will show and you will come across in a way that will again make the whole process easier.

There we are then. We are, I hope, agreed that you can be a more persuasive communicator and better negotiator if you work at it. Indeed, the process of trying itself will help you learn quicker and do better as a result. Continue this process for a while and you will be a match for anyone.

If this book sets you thinking in these terms, as well as giving you ideas on what techniques to develop it will have done its job.

So, at the risk of repetition, practice is the key.

Let me put it in another way. Do you want to get your own way more certainly, and more often? Do you want to reduce the friction of communication breakdowns at work? Do you want to be seen as a clear, authoritative communicator? A sensitive, and successful, negotiator?

Then bear in mind the principles set out here and give it a try. It will not go perfectly at first, but it will go better and better, and you will find you can do it and that it does work. That makes the practice, that is necessary, worthwhile.